TAROT

Landscape of the Soul

JEFF NEVES

To order additional copies of this book, contact:
Xlibris
844-714-8691
www.Xlibris.com
Orders@Xlibris.com

ISBN: Softcover   978-1-6641-5920-4
         Hardcover   978-1-6641-5921-1
         EBook   978-1-6641-5919-8

Library of Congress Control Number: 2021903561

Print information available on the last page.

Rev. date: 02/19/2021

For Lisa,

My love and my life

Contents

The Fool 1

The Magician 4

The Empress 9

The High Priestess 11

The Emperor 13

The Pope 15

Lovers 17

The Chariot 20

Justice 23

Strength 25

The Wheel: Prudence 27

Temperance: The Alchemist 29

The Play 31

The Hermit 34

The Hanged Man 36

Death 38

The Tower 40

The Devil 42

Judgement 45

The Star 47

The Moon 49

The Sun 51

The World 53

Preface:

Gilgamesh, Dorothy, and My Dinner with Andre'

"I want my stories to inspire day dreams in children,
because the imaginative child will become the imaginative man
or woman most able to create, to invent, and therefore to foster civilization."

L. Frank Baum

Gilgamesh leaves his position as ruler of Uruk and puts on animal skins to wander the world after the death of his companion Enkidu. This, oldest example of the "hero's journey," from around 1200 BC, is not an epic of the deeds of great gods and goddesses, but of a frail and flawed human who has lost sight of what his life should mean. Joseph Campbell, in his book "The Hero with a Thousand Faces," describes this story as being one of the great universal tales that occurs though out all cultures. Carl Jung labeled the themes that are present in these stories "archetypal;" basic ideas that identify what it means to be human. They are motifs that we all share as the essential make up of our psyche.

This book will be an attempt to discuss these tales using the Tarot as a center piece. The cards that were designed in the 14th century have fascinated and mystified people ever since their appearance in the towns of northern Italy. Over the past near 50 years, my study of the images has led me to examine myths, fairytales, art, philosophy, anthropology, and psychology. To get at the nut of what the cards offer we must go deep into our culture and our own minds, and draw on many sources to reach their essence. Gilgamesh, L. Frank Baum's Dorothy, and Wally and Andre' in their wonderful film "My Dinner with Andre'," will all be our guides on this journey, as will many of the myths and fairytales from various cultures around the world.

These stories are heretical in nature: they do not deal with the accepted ideas of philosophy and religion of every day life. They deal with shadow material and are the discourse of "fools". They lead us into the dark forest of the mind where shadows dance and the breeze whispers in our ear of secrets held in the night. The material presented in the Tarot can prepare us for that journey, which is the "vision quest:" search for knowledge of our truest self.

Twenty-seven thousand years ago, a lone child walked into a cave in the south of France, what we today call Chauvet. He or she carried a torch to light their way, touching it to the walls of the cave periodically to tap off the ash and probably to mark their path back. From the foot prints and two hand marks left, we think this child was about ten years old. Those prints are the only evidence that anyone had entered the cave for five thousand years. Before that, only the artist, who painted the animal figures on the walls themselves, are in evidence. That's as distant in the that child's past as the great pyramids in Egypt are to us. But it is very likely that the child would not have needed a Rosetta Stone to understand the symbolic language present in the cave. The culture that produced those images persisted for 20,000 years in that part of the world. From the thousand, or so, caves painted there are consistent themes that span that length of time. We have lost any key to understanding what the images of ibecks, lions, mammoths and elk meant to those people in those caves.

Reading the cards of the Tarot should be like, what entering the caves of southern France must have been for the Paleolithic people of thirty-two to twelve thousand years ago. It should be approached with a kind of reverence and as a ritual that offers a deeper meaning into our lives. It can become the thread we hold onto as we enter the labyrinth of the soul, that we may meet our inner selves and listen to our primal heart.

In the furthest reaches of Chauvet, is the image of a bison-man. This creature appears to be embracing the volva of a woman, whos' legs can be seen. Is this the marriage of the feminine power of nature with the male inclination to rule over that energy? It is hard not to draw parallels to the Minitour, despite the warnings from scholars that bison of that time were not domesticated. But the Minitour does wait in the dark reaches of ourselves. Are we prepared to encounter that part of ourselves?

Reading the Tarot should be like entering that cave and discovering scenes that depict the narrative of our life. We are being told a story fit for Fools.

Origins

Where did these cards come from and what was their purpose?

The earliest record of tarot cards is from the royal account book of Ferrara, Italy, in the year 1438 AD. This is the same year and place the Roman Catholic church brought together scholars from Constantinople, Alexandria and Rome for an ecumenical council to discuss church doctrine and establish the supremacy of the Pope in Rome. Trionfi, the original title of the deck and the game played with it, is really two decks of cards married into one: one of four suites, coins, cups, swords and wands, and one of usually twenty-two "trump" card that depict figures such as the Fool, Magician, Pope, Devil, Sun, Moon and World. The oldest surviving example of the deck is from the court of Duke Visconti in Milan, thought to have been painted in 1441in honor of the marriage of his daughter, Bianca Maria Visconti to Francesco Sforza, the mercenary captain of his forces. The trump cards are sometimes referred to as the "major arcana;" the word arcana meaning mystery. These cards seem to present a hierarchy of values or ideas that a person is meant to develop in the course of leading a spiritual life. However, there is no record of their use as anything other than the game called Trionfi. By 1500 the Italian nobles played a game called "tarocchi appropriate", where the players wrote poetic verse that corresponded to the cards they were dealt, about another in the group. In the second oldest deck we have, the Visconti-Sforza of 1450, each card has a hole in the top as if it had been pinned up somewhere.

The suit cards, often referred to as the minor arcana, probably came from the Moors who ruled Spain for several hundred years, although the Turks also had playing cards. To the Moors, the four suits represented the four classes of society: Cups, the clergy; Coins, the merchants; Swords, the ruling kings and their knights; and Wands, the peasanty or farming class. Today these suits are said to represent the concerns of daily life, rather than a social class. Coins are money, job and mundane matters, Cups are the emotional side of a person's life, Swords, stress and struggles in life, and Wands are concerned with personal growth and creativity. Cups and wands are a look to our inner life while coins and swords point to the outer social concerns.

To these suit cards from the Moors, the Italians of Milan, Florence and Urbino added various cards called Trionfi. In the game, these cards were valued according to their position in a hierarchy and "triumphed" over other cards of lower value. Many students of the cards, myself included, believe these trump cards represents a pictorial scheme of knowledge that would have been heresy in the eyes of the Church Fathers. The Inquisition was in full power at this point.

The late Gothic period (circa 1150-1500) saw an extraordinary influx of new ideas into Europe. Some came via Constantinople, as the silk road brought exotic foods, spices, and fabrics along with new ideas that perfumed the thoughts and dreams of people throughout Europe. But most ideas were carried as booty from the conquest of the first crusade in Spain. When the Caliph of Toledo, saw how King Alfonzo destroyed the first cities he encountered in the Moorish kingdom during the first crusade, he decided surrender would be the only way to save the great Mosque with its extraordinary library. This left the wealth of acquired knowledge of Muslim scholars open to the west. It not only included science, medicine, engineering treaties, but what we now think of as classical literature, philosophy, and mathematics of Greek and Roman minds, and ideas from Alexandrian theologians, and the Gnostics who had alternative visions of what Christianity meant.

As these books were translated into Latin, the language of European scholars, their influence spread through all classes of people. It sparked the romance of the troubadours, elevated and glorified the idea of womanhood, incited Alchemy's search for the "Anima Mundi" (which was the search for the soul of matter) and sparked a myriad of cults that mixed Gnostic Christianity, Zoroastrianism, and Sufi mysticism, in an attempt to discover the Kingdom of Heaven on earth. These new ideas were responsible for inspiring groups such as the Merovingians, Adamites, Taborites, Cathars, and Guglielmites. These groups threatened the authority of the Church which resulted in the establishment of the Inquisition. The followers of Saint Guglielma practiced a feminized version of Christianity and elected Maifreda da Piovano as the first female pope. In 1300 the Church charged 30 of her followers with heresy and Maifreda was burnt at the stake. Her portrait is said to appears as the "Popess" in the Visconti-Sforza (fig. 6) tarot deck. Could these cards have been a way of preserving a brand of knowledge that the Church disapproved of?

These musings will be an attempt to mix history with a personal view of these matters revealed in the cards. I do not claim to anything like a definitive interpretation, only a glimpse of what I have gleaned from 40 years of study, connecting the cards with myths, fairytales, alchemy and psychology, the "festival of the Fool" and Grail lore. Like any good story, we must find meaning that fits one's own life journey. My hope is that these cards can be clues to the path through the "Labyrinth of the Self."

The Parable of the House

You are born into the nursery of the house, and all of your needs are taken care of. You're fed, bathed and given an environment that enables you to grow and learn until you can begin to take care of yourself.

Gradually you start to learn about life. Moving to the library in this house, you become informed of the world and how things should work. But this knowledge is mostly second hand. You are rightly protected from the onslaught of the world.

The house is the "Psyche" or "Self." As you grow, your Ego inhabits more of this place. There is a front porch, which is the part of the Self visible to the world. It is not your true identity, but what you display to the world. It is comfortable and welcoming, but not truly who you are.

There is a parlor, a room of the house where you conduct your worldly business. Most acquaintances never go beyond this level of knowing who you are. In fact, many people never reach beyond this state of self-knowledge themselves, never venturing beyond the parlor's four walls and the window that looks out on the world.

Those who do explore beyond this point, may find the kitchen. This is where personal work is done. This is where the "Grounding Experience" happens. You get your hands dirty and begin to involve yourself with the raw stuff of life: earth, air, fire and water. This is where creativity comes into play and you begin to form something real. It may be in pottery, fiber art, poetry, music, painting or one of the many crafts. There is a garden outside this kitchen that acts as a source of your creativity and was, perhaps, where, in your youth, you played and could still feel magic in the world. With the garden and the kitchen, you bring something of yourself, vital and nourishing to the dining table to create a feast for those who are part of your inner circle; comrades in your search.

I call this experience the "wisdom of the kitchen" because so many of our fairytales have the hero living though this time. From the Russian Vasilisa, to Snow White, to Dorothy in "The Wonderful Wizard of Oz" (the book), many, especially female heroes, go through this time. It's when the hero, being trapped by a dark force, comes into contact with elemental forces that create life. The alchemists called this the "Prima Materia," base matter; the stuff one starts with. Most importantly it gets your head out of the stars and in touch with the Body Wisdom.

With time, you inhabit more of this house; the areas used to engage the outside world, porch and parlor; the rooms for family and close friends, dining room and upstairs; and areas for your personal growth, creative work, kitchen and garden. But you begin to become aware of strange things going on, sounds and stirrings beneath your feet: the basement.

Eventually you must answer the call and travel down into the dark and damp of the subterranean regions. In the basement you find the machinery and devices that maintain the house: furnace, plumbing and fuse box. Long neglected, this is also home to mice, spiders and perhaps a bat or two. Also are stored, chests with old discarded clothes and toys from a childhood, abandoned and forgotten. In one corner is an old work bench, dusty and neglected with rusted tools that once served a previous age. Perhaps once work was done in these dark regions of the Self. Confronting this area is mostly the challenge of midlife. There are many treasures to be discovered here, but if neglected much more than spiders will live in these shadows.

THE FOOL

01.Fool,Visconti-Sforza(c.1450)

02.Fool,Marseille(c.1550)

"There must be some way out of here,
Said the Joker to the Thief"
Bob Dylan

The Joker is all that remains in our modern playing cards of the Tarot trumps that began in the 15th century. The figure of the Fool, or Joker, is, quite literally the "wild" card. It can become any card, adopting its value or character. The Fool moves through the deck as the traveler journeys into the world, gleaning lessons from his wanderings. Percival, who was protected from knowledge of the world by his mother, began his quest to become one of Arthur's knights as the fool, innocent of the ways of the world and riding a donkey.

In medieval times, the fool played an integral part in the life of feudal society. The court jester, usually a dwarf or some poor individual with a mental or physical deformity, was afforded a place of honor next to kings and nobility. There was even the practice of intentionally deforming children to prepare them for a life in the aristocracy's homes, where they would be cared for throughout their lives. This person played the part, not only of comic relief, but was also given liberty to mock and criticize the nobility with impunity.

Spring festivals usually centered around the fool, he being a symbol of the rebirth of nature and its mad drive to procreate. These celebrations were thought to connect back to ancient Greek society and the "Greek Comedies." The plays, newly introduced to Medieval society from Arab translations, were associated with Dionysus celebrations: the god of fertility, wine and the ecstasy it brought. This god is directly associated with the Fool. He brought visions and insight into life that sober intellect failed to perceive.

Not seeing the world as "normal" people do, the fool is an outcast from society and must exist on its fringes. This idea is beautifully portrayed by Charlie Chaplin in his film "City Lights." The tramp, played by Chaplin, falls in love with a blind flower seller who thinks he is a rich aristocrat. He attempts to fulfill her image of this person through myriad mishaps and adventures. What is brought to light through the film is just how artificial and contrived these personas can be. At the time of his popularity the country was awash with immigrants who must have easily identified with the feeling of being in a strange and, at times, unwelcoming land.

The Fool often carries a wand with either a small mirror or a doll's head resembling his own. There's an interesting and hilarious play with this idea of mirror image in the Marx Brothers film "Duck Soup", where Groucho and Harpo test the idea of "are we the image we see or something else altogether?" How much of our inner self shows though?

Our earliest example of the Tarot Fool is from the Visconti-Sforza deck (fig.1) believed to be dated about 1450. The deck was probably commissioned to celebrate the crowning of Francesco Sforza as Duke of Milan. The barefoot figure, with ragged clothes and feathers stuck in his hair, has rather a dazed, vacant look on his face. He holds, slung over his right shoulder, a staff. His demeaner elicits our sympathy and is far from the jolly clown of later decks.

The Marseille Tarot deck, dated about 1550 and the first mass produced deck (using wood blocks), is where we first encounter the Fools companion, the dog (fig.2). It's very ambiguous whether the animal is helping or hindering this wanderer. Unlike the Visconti-Sforza Fool, he is on the move and has a satchel on the staff slung over his shoulder. In some versions the dog even seems to be tearing at the Fool's flesh, and he is oblivious. Is this creature the companion or foe of the traveler?

Arthur Waites' Fool, realized by the genius artistry of Pamela Coleman Smith, is about to step over a cliff, his gaze towards the stars. His dog is barking excitedly. Is it to warn him or adding to the confusion that is often associated with fools, clowns and jesters? Dionysus, often associated with the Fool card, is always accompanied by Satyrs, who are addicted to his wine and by the Maenads, who dress in fawn's skins. These women dance and drink themselves into ecstasy in honor of their god and his gifts from nature.

Perhaps the best example of the dog's role in the epic journey of the Fool, comes to us via the 1939 film version of L. Frank Baum's book, "The Wonderful Wizard of Oz." If we take this story metaphorically and see Dorothy as the ego's search for wholeness, Toto plays the part of energy bubbling up from the unconscious mind. This feature of the psyche is what the psychologist Carl Jung labeled the "Shadow." As young children we are indistinct from this instinctually, dynamic, playful self. It is seated in the body, our animal self, and has its' own wisdom irrespective of societies' norms. As we grow into our adult life this part of our self gets pushed further into darkness and becomes the Unconscious. We build our own Labyrinth to hide what is unacceptable to our conscious selves and society.

This is the situation Dorothy finds herself in, in Kansas, at the opening of the film. She is being ask to put away this part of herself and "find a place where she won't get into any trouble." Miss Gulch, playing the part of the "superego", what Freud saw as civilization's necessary limitations enforced on the Self, even wants to destroy Toto and rid everyone of this mischief maker. Dorothy finds herself stuck in the classic "wasteland," where all is barren and even mere survival is a desperate struggle. Symbolically this place is pushing her out. Toto, her creative child self, refuses to be suppressed. In this sense, the Fool's dog can be seen as the embodiment of the spirit of "foolery": sometimes chaotic, sometimes helpful, shocking us out of the mundane sleep walk we enact as a substitute for a full waking life.

Chaplin's "little tramp" is constantly coming up against the authority figure, usually in the guise of the police. The Fool lives forever outside the norm of society. He reveals to us just how thin are the masks we wear and tentative are the roles we play.

Perhaps the most recent example of the spirit of the Fool occurred with the hippie movement in the late 1960s. Calling themselves "freaks," they embraced clowning and poking fun at the society they rejected, and even at themselves.

The basic character of this card is Comedy. Even beset by tragic circumstances the Fool triumphs, and ends well. He is cloaked in innocence and filled with the soul of the child. He must now meet the guide who is both teacher and nemesis. He will cross paths with the Magician, the Thief.

When you meet the Fool, follow him, but only if you can maintain an innocent heart, and realize that falls will be part of your journey.

THE MAGICIAN

03. Magician, Visconti-Sforza (c.1450)

So, he took the cow's halter in his hand and off he started.
He hadn't gone far when he met a funny looking old man,
Who said to him, "Good morning Jack."
"Good morning to you," said Jack, and wondering how
He knew his name. "Well Jack, and where are you off to?"
"Oh, going to market to sell our cow here."
"Oh, you look the proper sort of chap to sell cows," said the man.
"I wonder if you know how many beans make five."
"Two in each hand and one in your mouth," said Jack, as sharp as a needle.
"Right you are," says the man, "and here they are, the very beans themselves…"

Joseph Jacobs
"Jack and the Beanstalk"

If the Fool is the beginning of the journey, then the Magician is the end. He is the wanderer who has come back to guide others on the path. In this sense he is the teacher, but not the benevolent guide or fostering elder. He has maintained his fool's character and is a "trickster." The Fool and Magician are two sides of the same coin: both outsiders, both estranged and indifferent to societies' norms.

The Magician is often associated with the Greek god Hermes: the messenger of the gods; the god of thieves, protector of travelers and the guide to souls on their way to the underworld. In the Norse tradition he would be the god Loki, who was responsible for the gifts given to the gods: Thor's hammer, Odin's staff. But he was also chief mischief maker.

In the Medieval morality plays, he can be seen as "the Vice," the invisible companion of the Devil who uses a "slapstick," two paddles of wood fastened together that made a loud crack when used, to aggravate "the Everyman." The "Punch and Judy" puppet show is a takeoff on these morality plays where the protagonist, Punch, beats his way out of trouble, even defeating the Devil himself in the end. The play traditionally begins, incidentally, with Punch unintentionally beating his neighbor's dog to death for being a barking nuisance. He is, like the Hercules figure of Greek mythology, always carrying things too far and letting his passions rule his behavior.

The movie version of "The Wizard of Oz" has Dorothy running away from home with Toto, only to meet Professor Marvel, a traveling performer, soothsayer and "man of miracles." She is taken in by his act, which he uses to convince her, through trickery, that she must go back home to her Aunt. But Dorothy is already caught up in the journey and discovers there is no going back. Once we cross over and take up our own cause, there is an explosion of energy that carries us away if we are not prepared. This is almost Dorothy's fate.

Western Judeo-Christian culture has all but done away with the character of the Magian-Trickster. We have replaced him with the "one true God." But still this character persists, certainly in the American Indian tales of Raven, Fox and Hare. The Egyptian Seth, plays this mythological role and the East is filled with tales of the "Monkey King."

The Russian "Baba Yaga" stories depict an old witch living in a house surrounded by the sculls of her victims that moves around the woods on chicken feet. She is extremely dangerous but very powerful and wise. She is just as likely to help travelers, as she is to devour them. The story of Vasilisa, a version of Cinderella, has the heroine, who serves Baba Yaga for a time, protected by a magic doll, a gift from her deceased mother. After performing three impossible tasks for the witch, she is granted the light (fire) she seeks because Baba Yaga recognizes her power. The doll acts as her source of protection, essentially an alter ego, much as the jester's image, a doll's head, is, atop his bauble. We could also say that Toto plays this role for Dorothy, although she receives additional protection once in Oz through having killed the Wicked Witch of the East and joining with the characters she meets on her journey. Toto both protects from and leads Dorothy into danger.

In Russia, there is also the tale of "The Fool," who wins the hand of the Tsars' daughter, with the help of his friends; the fastest man in the world, the strongest man in the world and the best shot on earth, who has sight that can see halfway around the globe. This same character gets transferred to Germany where he becomes the thief-trickster Baron Munchausen, who wins immortality in a duel, and has many outlandish adventures, even visiting the Moon. He eventually gives up eternal life in order to grow old and be with the woman he loves. Terry Gillian's film of the Baron has the hero in the late 1600s, "the age of reason," coming to terms with a world that no longer believes in heroes or their magical deeds.

The oldest version of the Magician card is from the Visconti-Sforza deck (fig.3), depicting an elderly bearded man, well dressed in red with a large hat. He is seated on a chest at a table that has a knife, a cup and two coins. He holds a wand in his left hand. His righthand hovers over some mysterious object: possibly a hat or satchel. He seems to be involved in some ritual. The oldest title of the card comes from a 1570 poem by Giovanni Susio, "il bagatto," meaning a trifle, which may refer to its low value in the game of Trionfi. This was the game the courts of northern Italy played using the cards in the late 1400s. It wasn't until the late 1700s that it was suggested that they may be connected to a mystical sect of knowledge, in a book by Gablin, before any notion of fortune telling was entertained. Until then, they were used only as a game, as far as we know.

The Magician of the 1500s from the Marseille deck, stands at a table with an array of objects, a knife and possibly some coins and two cups, as well as a few unidentifiable objects. In his left hand he holds a small wand, while his righthand hovers over the table. He seems well dressed, wearing what is sometimes called a "cap of maintenance": a broad brimmed hat often warn by shepherds. The figure is usually seen as performing a shell game; tricking gullible onlookers out of their hard-earned coin. Another early title for the card is the "Trivial Performer," which would seem to confirm his trickster identity.

The deck of the Tarot Marseille was the only deck known outside of northern Italy until about the 1890s. It being the first printed using wood blocks, was what writers such as Mathers, Papus, Crowley and eventually Waite, based their interpretation on: that and the idea the Tarot was connected to the Egyptian "Book of the Dead" (book of Thoth). The Jewish mystical sect of Kabbalah also played a part in forming their ideas. Arthur Waite's Tarot, illustrated by Pamela Coleman Smith, derives a large part of it's meaning from the Kabbalah's "Tree of Life." It is a diagram of ten spheres connected by 22 pathways which are interpreted by Waite as corresponding to the 22 cards of the major arcana.

Waite's Magician is elevated to that of divine teacher. He seems a man of power, having at his command all the emblems of the suit cards and holding a white wand high in the air. His other hand points towards earth. He is surrounded by vines and flowers. Gone is the idea of a trickster-guide, replaced by that of a prophet.

The prankster, guide, thief and protector of travelers, rattles the cage of our mundane lives, the role we place ourselves in, to lead us to a deeper existence. He steals the mask we wear in society to spur us on to a meaningful life. Once began, like Dorothy and Toto, we cannot go back home. Like Jack, five seemingly useless beans are all we have to go on.

When you meet the Magician, know he or she, will lead you on the road to finding who you truly are, but also know it is never a thing easily done and never what is expected.

Excavating the Labyrinth

I want to tell you a story. It's nearly forgotten, and yet persists. It huddles in the dark corners of our perception, just out of sight. It is ignored and denied, yet visits us in our dreams and nightmares. This story is about something dark and threatening, yet it can bring great beauty; the source of our creative energy. I want to tell you a story of the path through the Labyrinth and what waits for us there and how we meet it.

We have hidden, in shadow, a part of our self which we feel brings us shame, like Adam and Eve, realizing they are naked after eating the fruit of the tree of the knowledge of good and evil. They covered their naked bodies and so too we hide a side of ourselves in shame. At the center is the Labyrinth, our unconscious selves, and the Minotaur. Is this, as Morbius from the film "Forbidden Planet" calls it "the mindless primitive," "Monsters from the Id?"

The Minotaur is born of royal blood, but tainted with a curse. Minos the king of Crete, refused to sacrifice a white bull to Poseidon, traditionally his due. For this slight, Poseidon gave queen Pasiphae an unquenchable lust for this sacred beast and the Minotaur is the product of their union; a man with the head and horns of a bull. The master craftsman, Daedalus, was employed to build the labyrinth on Cnossus to hide the shame. He gave Pasiphae a magic ball of thread so she could enter and leave this maze at will.

But this is not a story of shame. There is an older story told of the Minotaur going back to the third millennium B.C. In those times, the union of the Queen Priestess, who represented the moon, put on cow horns and the Minos-king, wearing a bull's mask, were wed in a ritual under an oak. White bulls were sacred to the moon. Each king became the "moon-being" by this marriage of the Moon Priestess of Cnossos. This suggests an older agrarian culture was joined to a more patriarchal one as Crete was conquered by successive civilizations. The two societies found this way to live in harmony, but eventually the Greeks, who were said to dislike this marriage ritual, created this 'Minotaur in the Labyrinth" myth as a way of establishing once and for all the dominance of Greek culture and rule in the second millennium B.C. It is Theseus, one of the Athenian youths sent as tribute to be killed by the Minotaur, who eventually destroys the bull. The word Labyrinth comes from the Cretan word "labys", which was the double headed axe, the symbol of the two crescent moons, one waxing the other waning. This was the symbol of the king's sovereignty.

We, like those ancient Greeks, have created a labyrinth to hide our baser selves, our primal heart. Carl Jung called this part of ourselves the Shadow. It is the ancient instinctual part of who we are, as well as memories and feelings we don't deal with in the here and now. What tribute do we send into the darkness to keep this bargain? What do we sacrifice in life to maintain our civilized selves? Joseph Campbell said we need not take this journey into the maze of the Self alone. Many have traveled the path before us and we can follow their thread. I believe the Tarot is such a guide leading us to meet our Shadow Self and eventually integrating it into a richer life. Does the cost of living in a technologically advanced society, enjoying the gifts of Daedalus, who also made toys for the king's children, mean we must hide a dark part of ourselves in the Labyrinth of the Soul? Is that truth so horrible and the cost so high we must eventually destroy the beast?

The image of the Minotaur goes way back. Bull cults have persisted throughout the Mediterranean region over time. Sometimes they represent the sun's power, reign and majesty, bringing both clear sight and conscious action. Other times they are identified with the moon, speaking of life's mysteries and the Earths regenerative cycles; dying and renewing itself. The man-bull figure may even go back to the beginning of humans attempt to record their thoughts and feelings in the thirty-two-thousand year old cave paintings of Chauvet.

What I hope to address in these writings is how the hidden parts of ourselves can be approached through the use of a deck of ancient cards. The ideas presented there are universal themes, what Carl Jung called "archetypal" and ring out in myths, legends and fairy tales. We need not enter the labyrinth alone. We can carry the thread of Pasiphae to guide our way in the search for our Primal Heart. This is the "Vision Quest" we are on. In it, we must ultimately meet our Minotaur in order to create a life that is vital and whole. Who knows what other phantoms, wonders or allies we will meet in that maze? One thing is certain, it is ourselves we approach there in the shadows. To meet this hidden part of the Self is the challenge of one who wants to be truly alive and fully engaged in creating a life.

This is not about fortune telling, but about story telling. We are a race of story tellers. It's how we define ourselves as individuals and our people as a civilization and their place in the cosmos. It informs our past, gives us this present and presents a plausible future. In ancient times, these myths were enacted through rituals that brought the community together. They danced, played music, beat drums, chanted to the gods and the stories were made real and a connection was established. It became a reality. Now we attend theatre, dance, music and art exhibits, but we have lost a visceral connection to Story.

This book will be a guide in an attempt to re-establish a connection through the Tarot, cards that depict one of the most basic and essential tales known to humankind. One that goes back as far as Gilgamesh's search for answers to life's mysteries; Isis' wandering quest for her murdered lover, Osiris; Psyches' trials to regain her companion Eros; Percival's quest for the Grail; or a young Theseus' journey though the labyrinth.

The cards depict a story that is, at its heart, Comedy. For this is the tale of the Fool. Like Shakespeare's fool in "King Lear", he saves us from an insane world. Hamlet does not have the benefit of this figure and perhaps this is one reason he ends in tragedy. "Alas, poor Yorick, I knew him Horatio, a fellow of infinite jest, of most excellent fancy, he hath borne me on his back a thousand times...."

How does the story begin? Like all stories, in darkness and a journey into light and it's stabbing pain and then a mother's gentle embrace and succoring nourishment. We are born in innocence and must journey into the world to know pain, joy, love and rejection. I believe these cards can begin to unravel this mystery of life and present us with the central narrative that we are to live. Existence is a mystery to be experienced, not a puzzle to be solved. But we need a guide through the tumult that is the world.

How does the story begin? With a King too righteous and harsh for his people to bear, so they procure a mate, his equal, who comes from the wild. Or with a simple miller who boasts of his only daughter, most beloved in the world, that she possesses the ability to spin straw into gold. Or with a ruler who foolishly invites all but one fairy to the christening of his daughter. Or with a poor couple, childless, and the wife longing to taste an onion she spies in her neighbor's garden. Loss and discontent propel the journey into the dark forest, even when sanity warns us "stay away."

The search is a quest to find a place in a narrative that connects us to the world, with all that it offers, both good and bad, suffering and joy, yin and yang. Human life has no intrinsic meaning, it is we who infuse meaning into it. We create a life that has resonance in the cosmos. In the past, societies had myths that established a communal identity. They enacted those stories through rituals. Modern life is devoid of such values. Change seems to be our only constant. What can we hold onto?

When King Arthur's knights went on a quest, they entered the forest at some unknown point, without a clear path. This seems to be the lot of anyone on the Vision Quest in today's society. I am proposing that these cards can at least be a map and guide to fulfillment. Though alone, we have a powerful ally. The thread of Ariadne will lead us through the maze of the Self.

THE EMPRESS

04.Empress Charity,Visconti(c.1441)

But first we must tell of how the story began, with Mother and Father and the keeper of the mysteries and the high priest of ritual. These are represented by the next four cards:

The Empress, High Priestess, Emperor, and Pope. They are the four corner stones of the psyche; our sense of self that is given by family and culture. They set the stage for how we will relate to the world on the beginning of the journey. These four cards are the Foundation Cards and support everything we build on in our lives.

I am taking the cards slightly out of their traditional order, in order to present a discussion of the thematic ideas that run throughout. The general order is maintained, although some decks rearrange the numerical sequence differently from the oldest source, the Susio poem of the late 1500s, in order to fit one philosophical scheme or another. The major arcanum does follow a basic chronological sequence from childhood, youth, adulthood and to elder. The point, though, is that any card can have an influence in any of life's episodes, especially these foundation cards that represent early life development.

Our first contact with the world is of Mother. Even before birth we are aware of her voice and beating heart. She is our entire universe and brings life and sustenance. This is the essence of the Empress card. On a grand scale, she is "Mother Earth" who sustains us all. The Greeks identified her as Demeter, goddess of fertility and the harvest, specifically wheat. She was the central figure in the Eleusinian cult practiced in ancient Greece. The rituals enacted there by the initiates involved the birth of a divine child and savior. Like wheat, he was born of the earth, the mother. He was laid in a manger and his flesh was eaten by his followers in the form of bread. His blood was drunk in the form of wine.

"Meter" means mother and "De" is the Greek letter delta, a triangle. This sign is called the "letter of the Vulva," a triangle, symbolic of the passage way through which mother delivers life into the world. This image goes all the way back to man's first symbolic representations, seen in the cave paintings in Chauvet, at the deepest part of this beautiful cathedral of early humans. There seemed to be great reverence placed on this symbol.

In the late gothic period of Europe, the "Cult of Mary" stood as a powerful metaphor through which people could approach the all-powerful God. She was, after all, human and as portrayed as "Madonna and Child," became the emblem of mercy and grace who could intercede for us with God, the omnipotent ruler.

The oldest image of the Empress card is from the Visconti deck (fig.4, c.1441) depicting a crowned Queen holding a chalice like object in her right hand and embracing a naked child suckling her breast, in her left. Beneath her feet is a bearded man in robes and crown, quizzically looking out at us. His left hand is raised as if in a greeting. The Empress seems to be gazing down at him. This card was originally one of the three "Divine Virtues" cards: Faith, Hope and Charity: she being the later. There is, in this oldest deck, an actual Empress card, but I believe the essence of what has come to be todays' Empress is taken from the Charity card; a spirit of loving benevolence. She is the original life-giving force of existence.

When the Empress is encountered, you must open yourself to her grace and accept her guidance. Be nourished and refreshed, but know that she is leading you on to a deeper existence. Demeter nursed the king's son Demophon on her search for her daughter Persephone, and tried to give him the gift of immortality by burning off his mortal self in the hearth. We too must burn in that fire in order to achieve our goals, nourished by the Empress.

THE HIGH PRIESTESS

05.Popess,Visconti(c.1441)   06.Popess,Visconti-Sforza(c.1450)

As a small child grows, their perspective takes in more of the world. The scope of awareness begins to be more than just that of the loving mother. Very young children do not make the distinction between the world outside of them and their inner self. Their identity rests in their perceptions of inner thoughts and feelings, mixed with the world around them. I call this the "Dream Time;" living in a world infused with one's own living soul. The ego, as a distinct entity from the environment, has not yet been forged in the kiln of life. To this small child monsters and angels exist because they live in the landscape of the psyche. The mystery of life is open to them and dreams both beautiful and disturbing embrace and rule their lives.

When I was about four years old, my aunt used to take me to the park. We would spend our days wandering around the zoo, the duck pond and the gardens. She more or less let me explore the grounds as I wished. The formal gardens were my favorite and I would be enthralled, as I ran around, what to me, was a magical kingdom. It stands as a vision of the world more beautiful and filled with wonders, than I have rarely ever known since. What was open to that child's mind is now veiled in mystery. My adult sense of me as distinct from the world has cut off that experience of the world.

The experience of the Dream Time is the essence of the High Priestess. We enter this reality each night in dreams, where life is once again a vast mystery. The High Priestess sits before a veil that hides a watery landscape, only vaguely perceived. She acts as the Sphinx, barring entrance unless we answer her riddle. She is queen of the night and the moon is her emblem. Persephone, the Greek goddess of the underworld, is her sister. Cloaked in mystery, she is Arthur's witch sister, Morgan le Fay, both wonderous and overwhelming.

Bruno Bettelheim, in his book "The Uses of Enchantment" discusses the idea of the Stepmother. From the perspective of the child, when mother, the loving all giving person, begins to say "no," and sets boundaries for the good of the growing child, she is no longer the person they once knew and must have been replaced by someone pretending to be mother. She becomes the "Stepmother." This idea is closely aligned with the figure of the trickster: mother is preparing the youth for the world, contrary to their preferences and desires.

The oldest example of this card is from the Visconti deck (fig.5) and depicts the second of the three Divine Virtues: Faith. She is seated wearing a golden crown with her right hand raised in a blessing. Beside her floats a chalice. Her left hand holds a tall cross. Below her is, again, the crowned figure looking out at us. This may represent the triumph of virtue over worldly affairs.

The second example is from the Visconti-Sforza deck (fig.6), probably commissioned to celebrate the crowning of Francesco Sforza as duke of Milan after the death of Filippo Visconti in 1450. The card is named "Popess," a companion to the Pope card. She wears a three-tiered crown, like the Pope, and holds a tall staff topped by a cross in her right hand, and a closed black book in her other. Her gown is not that of the office of Pope, but rather, that of a nun. It has been speculated that this is meant to be a portrait of Sister Manfreda, who lived about 150 years earlier and was a distant cousin of the Visconti family. She was elected Pope by her peers, the Gugliemites, and then condemned and burnt at the stake by the Inquisition.

This version of the card began as "Faith" is transformed to the "Popess" and eventually becomes the "High Priestess." It presents the archetype of a woman of power who holds in her hand a book or, in the Waite-Smith deck, a scroll with the word "Tora" visible, knowledge that is not given but realized through life's journey. She presents life as a mystery and, as one of the four corner stones of the psyche, presents this existence as a time of wonders to be experienced.

The step-mother, for her identification as evil, is the catalyst who throws us into the world. Arthur's knights, embarking on a quest, would enter the wood at the point without a any sure path, that they should be at Fates' mercy. We start our lives at the point without a clear path. We journey into the night lit only by the reflected light of the moon, where things are perceived, not as they are, but as projections of our inner hopes and fears. We walk this world to realize the Self we truly are. That is our challenge!

Upon meeting the High Priestess, know that her secrets are not given to just any traveler. Open your soul to her and let her words guide you to the next stage of your quest. She knows your heart.

THE EMPEROR

6b. Emperor, Visconti-Sforza (c. 1450)

But we must also prepare for the "Quest." Like Percival, who meets up with his uncle and is taught the ways of chivalry, we must be taught the ways of the world. The young child begins to know Father: The Emperor. This is Animus, the male side of the psyche according to Carl Jung. He, unlike Anima, Mother, can come from many sources other than one's actual father. Teachers, coaches, Rabbis, all may offer this knowledge to the child, sharing their experience of life.

The Emperor is the law giver and rules by force of will. He represents the status quo; the way society operates, the order of the mundane. But he can also be seen as the Green Knight who comes to Arthur's court and lays a challenge to any knight to cut off his head, and then meet him in one years' time to receive a blow by his sword. This is met by Gawain who quests for one year and is then tested by the ladies of the castle. He proves his loyalty and virtue but wears a magic girdle that will keep him from harm. Because of this, he receives

13

a light wound from the Green Knight for this minor transgression. The Emperor is the one, in the guise of the Green Knight, who prepares and sends us into the world to fulfill our quest. In medieval England this Green Knight was considered a form of the "Green Man," the antlered huntsman, Herne. He represents the ways of the forest and nature's laws, not societies.

The Emperor is also Zeus, the sky god, who's emblem is the eagle. This shows up in the Visconti-Sforza (fig.6b) Tarot on the Emperor's crown and was also the sign of the Holy Roman Emperor. There is also an Empress in this deck; the king's counterpart. I believe that the "Charity" card, though, already discussed, more correctly identifies the architype of the Empress, in modern decks.

The Visconti deck is fascinating in its feminist attitude. Not only is the Empress, Charity and Faith, the Popess, all women, but the Chariot, Strength, Star and World cards all have female figures. In fact, this deck also has a female knight in each suit, along with the male. Perhaps this is not surprising knowing what we do about the late Gothic period in Europe. The cult of Mary and courtly love, where the woman took the lead in choosing who was to serve her, along with the poetry of the troubadours honoring the ideal of womanhood, all represented this idealization of womanhood. In the south of France, the Valentinian Christians required each man to protect and honor a specific woman for a years' time. That man's name was drawn by the woman from a bowl at random at a yearly ceremony in the spring. The practice continued for more than a century until it was stopped by the Inquisition.

The Emperor's attitude towards the world is one specifically male. Men, from my experience, get most of their identity from "what they do." This involves work, hobbies and status they hold in society. Teams, possessions and bank accounts can also come into play. We seem to be hard wired with our focus outward. Women seem to get their sense of self from "who they are." This involves emotions, feeling and intuitions. Relationships, friends and family also play an important part for women. Their focus is inward. This is not to say, there aren't men who have these sensibilities and women who derive an identity from their jobs and status in society, but in general my experience tells me we tend to look at life in these ways. It is traditionally the man's, the Emperor's, job to introduce the child to the ways of the world, but today's world demands we open this role to both men and women so we see life not just as one thing or the other.

In the Waite-Smith deck, the Emperor seems to be severe and a bit lonely. Does it have to be only this stern attitude taken towards life? We need both Emperor and Empress as well as High Priestess' sense of wonder and mystery to influence our lives. Carl Jung asserted that each man carries with him the anima, which comes primarily from mother, and each woman, the animus, coming from father figures. The challenge is to integrate this other side of our self into daily life.

When the Emperor is encountered listen to his lessons and derive strength from his counsel that you will be prepared for the long journey ahead.

THE POPE

07. Pope, Visconti-Sforza (c. 1450)

    So, we turn to the final corner stone of the child's influences: the Pope; "Ritual." The oldest version of this card that has survived, is in the Visconti-Sforza deck (fig.7). It pictures a bearded man seated with the three teared Papal Crown. In his right hand is a golden rod or spear and his left hand is raised in a benediction, or blessing. His gown is all white and he has a cloak with the golden sun insignia all over. The interior of the cloak is green. He is clearly the leader of the faithful and like Peter, the "rock" upon which Christ built his church, watches over his flock. (It should be noted that the pope was not declared to be "infallible" in church matters until the Vatican Council of 1870.)

    Modern decks, including the Waite-Smith, have renamed this card the "Hierophant," in an attempt to connect it with Mediterranean mystery sects of ancient times. The title represented a priest or priestess in Greece, where the Eleusinian Mysteries and the Oracle at Delphi were practiced. Demeter, the Great Mother of fertility, was a focus of these sects. Her search for her daughter, abducted by Hades, was thought to be a metaphor for the soul's journey through life.

This card represents the established body of knowledge that points to things sacred: those beyond the mundane or day to day. Unlike the High Priestess, who presents the wonder of life and its secrets just out of reach, the Pope offers us "Ritual" to approach those hidden things. The rites, symbols and myths (story) become a means to initiate an individual to a deeper meaning of life.

The Pope is closely aligned with the Greek god Apollo, representing the full light of the sun and the clear seeing intellect. He was also the god of art and music. As such he represents all of culture that strives to bring meaning to human life. This includes the arts, theatre, religion, philosophy, music and science. Each is a specific discipline that approaches the wonder of existence from a different angle, answering specific questions and ignoring others. Science asks "how" does the universe operate, where religion asks "what" is the purpose of human life? This corner stone of the child's psyche is derived from the teachings of one's culture. It is obtained from religion and schooling, and in today's world, from movies, books and television.

Like the Fool and Magician, or the Emperor and the Empress, the Pope is one side of a coin representing the way through to the mysteries of life, with the other side, in this case, being the High Priestess. The Waite-Smith deck of 1909 seems to express this connection by having both figures, High Priestess and Hierophant, seated between two pillars. In the case of the High Priestess the pillars are labeled with the letter "B" on one and "J" on the other. This is said to stand for Boaz; mercy and Jachin; severity, the two influencing spirits in the practice of the Golden Dawn, the secret society to which both Arthur Waite and Pamela Coleman Smith belonged.

These cards, numbered II though V in modern decks, make up these four corner stones that become the foundation of a person's mind and personality. They come early in life and are with us though out our journey. They are the basis for the formation of the ego, which is our conscious identity. Its why psychoanalysis has such a large focus on childhood. To know these elements is to know the source of personhood.

When you meet the Pope on your quest, listen intently to his counsel, but do not linger long by his side, that your journey ends there and ritual becomes an empty performance. Stay true to the stirrings of the heart.

LOVERS

08.Lovers, Visconti(c.1441)

8b.Lovers,Marseille(c.1550)

8c.Lovers,Waite(c.1909)

"All I really, really want our love to do,
is to bring out the best in me and in you, too."
Joni Mitchell

The next two cards, the Lovers and Chariot, are transitional cards. They represent moving from one stage of life to the next. In this case the progression is from the world of the family, home and societies tutoring to one's own sense of self as being separate from those things: developing the Ego, that can stand on its own. In modern times this seems to be adolescence through the early twenties; a time when the youth discovers who they are and what path their life will take. Traditional societies, such as native Americans, had rituals and initiation ceremonies to guide the individual to their rightful place in the tribe. Today there seems to be little guidance for youths on the road to adulthood. They must find their own way. The Amish, a traditional society all their own, even designate a period of time called "rumspringa," when the teen leaves the home and experiences the "English" or modern world. It is a period filled with many dangers and some few do not survive. During this period, a youth is thrown into the world and permitted to experience those things that were forbidden in the shelter of the Amish community. The hope is that they will then choose to rejoin the group voluntarily.

This time can be a flowering of the self and represents one of life's most beautiful periods. It is when one finds a "significant other," who draws out of them all that is good and true. The late middle ages were the dawn of romantic love and some scholars, Joseph Campbell included, would say also the birth of the "individual;" one who determines their own destiny. This was exquisitely expressed in the Arthurian legends and in the romance stories such as "Tristan and Iseult." The troubadours were perhaps the most effective catalyst for spreading these ideas, which may have originated with Arab and Persian love poetry.

The oldest version of the Lovers in the tarot is from the Visconti deck (fig.8) and is thought to represent the marriage of Francesco Sforza to Bianca Maria Visconti the only off spring of the duke of Milan, Filippo Maria Visconti. They grasp each-others hands standing under an umbrella with the Visconti coat of arms on it. A small gray hound, a symbol of fertility, lies at their feet. A blindfolded winged Cupid (Eros) hovers above, holding an arrow in each hand pointed at the lovers. The god Eros was said to have two types of arrows in his quiver: a gold tipped one that caused infatuation and a lead tipped one that caused loathing. The figure of Eros shows up in most versions of the Lovers card and represents the piecing all-encompassing passion that overtakes a person in love.

This passion is beautifully expressed in the Greek myth of Eros and Psyche. The human maiden, Psyche, was so beautiful that worship of Aphrodite almost completely ceased. The goddess asked Eros to have Psyche fall in love with some old ugly man, but when he saw her beauty, he fell in love. He began to visit her in her bed at night, where their love was consummated. Psyche never saw her lover on these visits and her father consulted the oracle of Apollo and was told that Psyche's lover was a serpent.

Psyche had grown to love the unseen visitor of the night, but feared the oracle might be true. She lit a lamp one night when Eros had fallen asleep and beheld one so beautiful that in her ecstasy let a drop of hot oil from the lamp fall on the sleeping Eros, waking him and causing him to disappear.

This begins Psyche's epic quest to find her lover, where Aphrodite assigns her three tasks to fulfill before she succeeds in her search. First is to separate a mixed heap of grain, where she is helped by some accommodating ants. Then she must gather fleece from a flock of wild sheep. She picks it from reeds that the sheep go through, and finally she must collect water from the source of the river Styx which surrounds the land of the dead, where she is helped by an Eagle.

This epic journey is one of many that mirror the ideas behind the trumps of the tarot. A quest must be taken on in order to find one's fulfillment. Aphrodite demands one last task of Psyche: to descend into Hades and bring back a container of some of Persephone's beauty. When she obtains the container, her curiosity gets the better of her and she opens it to find it holds "Sleep." Eros finds her and replaces it back in the container.

We have in this story many of the classic elements that define the search for "Self." Submitting to the service of one more powerful is in many of the fairytales that were passed mother to daughter as an oral tradition. The service is almost always of a menial nature but one that brings the subject into contact with the basic elements of life itself. The Grimm's brothers "Iron Hams" becomes a gardener in the king's palace; "Cinderella" serves her step mother and step sisters tending the hearth; "Snow White" cooks and cleans for the seven dwarfs; the "Goose Girl" tends the flock of the king's geese. This act of service is called the "Grounding Experience" and is necessary to the success of finding a balance in one's life.

The Lovers card brings up the tradition established in the 12th century of courtly love. It was once thought that this was merely a sort of game played by the nobility. It now seems that it was much more than that throughout the late Gothic period. The woman, usually of noble birth, was in charge of deciding whether a knight's service would be accepted on her behalf. Often the knight was of a lower class, perhaps a merchant's son made out with armor to fight one of the many small wars that broke out among the provinces. The woman was also in charge of how far the relationship would go. It seemed many of these arrangements often were love affairs, but she was always the one deciding how and how far it progressed. Marriage was a social contract for the mutual benefit of the two families involved. Love had nothing to do with it.

The Marseille tarot (fig.8b) shows a scene called "the judgement of Paris." It's the story of the wedding of Thetis, a sea goddess, to Peleus, a mortal. The god Eris, god of discord, was not invited to the festivities. (Of course, why would anyone invite discord to their wedding?) As a result, Eris tossed a golden apple in amongst the guests and said it belonged to the "fairest of them all." This began an argument among Hera, Athena and Aphrodite as to who should own the treasure. Zeus chose a shepherd boy, Paris, to judge the rightful beauty. Hera told Paris she would make him king of all Asia, if he chose her. Athena said she would make him victorious in every battle. Aphrodite settled the matter by unclasping her girdle where Eros was hiding and shot a gold tipped arrow into Paris. Of course, she won and promised him the most beautiful woman on earth, Helen, who was married to Menelaus, king of Sparta, and so, because of vanity and Eros' arrow we have the Trojan War. It seems we never learn.

The Waite-Smith deck (fig.8c) tries to elevate the scene to that of primordial love between Adam and Eve, before the Fall. They stand naked with Eve before the "tree of the knowledge of good and evil," with the snake wrapped around it. Adam stands before the "tree of eternal life" as a winged figure floats above the two lovers. This is meant to be, I believe, innocent and pure love: first love. Waite's idea behind the Lovers card presents more of an icon rather than an experience, like that presented in the Visconti deck; an actual scene from a wedding.

The Lovers card is a time of moving from the domain of the parent's home and society's establishments to a broader experience of the world. Love finds us drawn into the life of another, even valuing that life over our own. The challenge is to integrate who we are with who they are and will become. We rarely perceive the true nature of that "other" without many years of dedicated work, listening and opening up ourselves to this new found love. This is the first of many transitions life has to offer. One that necessarily entails becoming vulnerable to another person. In this sense, it has a lot in common with the Fool card. Being "in love" is often referred to as being one's fool.

THE CHARIOT

09.Chariot,Visconti(c.1441)

9b.Chariot,Waite(c.1909)

Moving from the tutelage of parents and school into the broader realm of the world is the domain of the "Chariot." Where the Lovers card is a move into self-knowledge through opening ourselves to another, the Chariot is a move out into the society, finding our place in it. In the Marseille deck we view a youth decked out in armor on a chariot drawn by two horses. He is crowned and holds a long scepter and the face of one of two moons is on each shoulder. Waite's figure (fig.9b) is similar, showing regal strength and determination, as the charioteer moves away from the walled city into the unknown, drawn by one white and one black sphinx. On the front of his vehicle is a winged circle and the lingam-yoni (for male-female) symbol. There is a sense here that life is propelled by both positive and negative forces. He is fashioned with all that society can provide. This is traditionally a time when the youth joins the work force or the military and begins a family life. Waite has him decked out as the warrior ready to make his mark in society.

There is a close association here with Ares, the Greek god of war, who is always accompanied by Eris, god of discord, Phobos, fright, and Deimos, panic. This is the severe side of the Chariot, but there is an older version of the card in both Visconti (fig.9) and Visconti-Sforza decks. They both have a crowned woman in the chariot drawn by white horses. The older Visconti version has her holding a disk with the family emblem of a dove. Her gown is decorated with laurel and palm leaves and the ducal crown. The Visconti-Sforza is similar except the radiant sun adorns her gown and she holds an orb before her. The horses are winged.

These two older renditions of the card call to mind Athena, the goddess of strategy in war and seem to express the idea of the triumphant parade that followed a successful campaign of the Roman legions, returning to the capitol city. These pageants were called Trionfi which many believe to be the inspiration for Tarot cards. The poet Petrarch wrote an allegorical epic poem with the same name, which dramatized the idea that virtue can triumph over vice. The poem was the only one written by the author in the native Italian, not the scholar's language of Latin. Written in 1375, it leads one through love, chastity, death, fame, time and eternity.

Perhaps todays meaning for the card lies in the combination of the two versions. Robert Bly, the poet and writer on the meaning of fairy tales, talks about the modern warrior as being someone who goes into the board meeting and demands that ethical behavior on the part of the company should win over pure profit motive. If one stands up to fight that battle, they had better be prepared for the ensuing tumult; a warrior.

The Chariot leads one into the main stream of life and society. The armor of the warrior is the established Ego that has developed over the years. This Ego, a sense of the person as a unique individual in charge of their own destiny, is now challenged to integrate itself into society. The initiate now enters the realm of the Four Cardinal Virtues (the four cards after the Lovers card.) Their lessons must be garnered from a life lived with knowledge and determination. With the gifts of the culture possessed by the youth, they enter the status quo of family, work, politics and a community of close friends and casual associates. Life pulls on all sides and confronts each with various demands. This is the "field of action" that one must engage in that the ego conscious identity is challenged to become a part of and, at the same time, remain true to oneself.

When the Chariot is encountered, know you are called to leave the safety and comfort of your set way of life. The warrior's armor must be worn: nothing in life worth having is given without cunning and daring and sometimes a battle.

The Minor Arcanum

The deck of cards that was adopted from the Moors, who ruled Spain from the 8th century through the 15th, was of four suits: coins, cups, swords and wands. The twenty-two major arcanum cards (trumps) were added to it by the Medieval peoples of northern Italy. The four suits were said to represent the four classes in gothic society. Coins represented the merchant class; cups the clergy; swords the ruling kings, queens and knights; and wands the peasantry, the farming class. Their meaning has transposed to modern life to represent the four concerns that confront living in today's world.

Coins: money, work, mundane matters and providing for the basic concerns of living.

Cups: love, emotions and intuitions; the pleasures and enjoyments in life but also unease and feelings of loneliness and depression.

Swords: stress and struggle; conflict and dealing with authority, as well as taking a stand.

Wands: your personal work (tending your garden) and growth; art, craft, music.

Until Pamela Coleman Smith's rendering of Arthur Waite's ideas for a modern tarot deck, published by the Ryder Co. in 1909, no set of the cards fully illustrated the suits, as far as we know. According to reports, Waite was very specific in the layout and design of the 22 trump cards but was much less so with the suit cards. Ms. Smith was more or less free to design them as she saw fit. Thankfully she was not only a brilliant illustrator but also a talented story teller. She published two volumes of "Annancy Stories;" Jamaican folk tales, where she lived as a child for several years. She also illustrated several periodicals from time to time. The depictions she designed for the suits of the tarot have a strong element of storytelling to them. The trumps, on the other hand, stand more as icons or symbols. The origins of her ideas are unknown to us, but she was an artist who experimented with music and seeking mystical visions. The occult society of the Golden Dawn, whose members include Waite and Aleister Crowley and many artist and theatre people of the time, also played a large part. Basic to their thinking were the teaching of the Cabala; a Jewish mystical sect.

The scheme of the suits, the numbered sequence, seems to follow the ideas inherent in numerology.

One: is wholeness, beginning, the essence of that suit.

Two: balance, passive, stable, a still point.

Three: co-operative action, movement, progress, realization.

Four: stable, restive, completing a cycle.

Five: unrest, confusion, difficulties, out of sorts.

Six: the antithesis of five, or its answer, home, harmony.

Seven: unrest, the unknown, unease.

Eight: the next step, conclusion, answer to seven, achievement.

Nine: stable, no movement, secure, completion.

Ten: the ultimate conclusion of that suit, finality.

This seems a general overview of the cards with the Page, student; Knight, journeying forth, the quest; Queen, ruling from an inner strength; King, power of will.

The four cardinal virtues are the next four cards considered in the major arcanum and their lessons must be heard before the initiate can proceed with the journey. They usually reveal themselves in the beginning of adult life; where one begins to integrate the Ego into society at large.

JUSTICE

10. Justice, Visconti-Sforza (c.1450)

The first of the carnal virtues is Justice. Carnal, because unlike the divine virtues, Faith, Hope, and Charity, which are gifts from God according to the church of the middle ages, Justice is realized and established from the works of man. In the Visconti-Sforza (fig.10), Marseille and Waite-Smith decks, Lady Justice is seated with a sword in her right hand and scales in the left. This figure is not blindfolded. She represents the clear vision of the intellect illuminating the world for what it is and is associated with the Greek goddess Themis, daughter of Gaia, the earth mother and Ouranos, sky father. Themis means "natural law" and as such represents the way life works.

Human life is an arrangement that ignores our civilized sensibilities. On the most basic level we are life eating life, literally. We live by consuming the living energy of other creatures, whether they be plant or animal. There is no getting around this reality even if one adopts veganism. We live on the life of others. This arrangement of the natural order is absolutely unavoidable and may be why we surround the act of eating with so many rituals: it is a communal act, at a table with utensils involving a set of manners. We seek to elevate it above the simple and animal act of consuming another's life.

Societally, my good fortune may be at the cost of somebody else's. I am sitting rather comfortably in my house, well fed and clothed but many in this world are not so blessed. I could sell everything and give it to the poor; it has been done before; think of Saint Francis or Mother Theresa. We could open the vaults of the world and distribute the wealth throughout the populace, there have been attempts, but none seem able to correct the faults inherent in our systems of economics or right greed and corruption. There is enough food on earth to feed everyone, but still many go hungry. Surely, I can do more than I do and so, too, our governing institutions. It disturbs me to think, in the words of Jesus, "the poor will be with you always." Perhaps this is the real meaning of "Original Sin:" Original, because it is an inescapable part of the human condition I am a part of. Justice speaks to a realization of life's inequities but, I believe, also a desire to act positively; not simple complacency to the world's shortcomings.

The Justice card recognizes that to participate in the society of man is to perceive the evil done; wrongs inflicted on the less fortunate: injustice, ignorance and inequality. We don't have to participate in the drama that is this world. We can live in a cloister or hermitage, but I believe the challenge is to say yes to the world, trying to do good when possible. We can strive to leave this earth better than we found it.

Justice is associated with the suit of Swords, which is the ruling class of kings, queens and knights: the authority and rule of Law that holds society together. But it is also represents chivalry and righting the wrongs of the world. The scales this figure holds are the attempt to balance an idealistic outlook of utopian goals against an opposite cynical attitude of giving in to the status quo: "dog eat dog." Stoicism seems to come closest to balancing engagement in life with a positive outlook and not falling into utter despair. "Mental habits harmonizing with reason and the natural order of things." Cicero. Taking up the sword of Justice is to see clearly the world as it is and accept our place in it without despair or illusions.

STRENGTH

11. Strength, Visconti-Sforza (c.1450)   12. Strength, Visconti (c.1441)

Once the clear light of Justice illuminates the world, and is accepted, then action must take place in the drama of the world. The Strength card is associated with the suit of Coins, which represented the merchant class in medieval society: commerce and trade. Money is a vehicle for engagement in society. It is the symbol of action in the field of time played out in society and culture.

In the beginning of the Hindu holy book, Bhagavad Gita, prince Arjuna sees from his chariot the faces of his relatives and friends in the line of the opposing army, just before the battle is about to take place. He breaks down and declares to his friend, Krishna, that he cannot enter a battle knowing it will result in the death of his close friends and family. Krishna, the Hindu equivalent of the Christian Jesus, explains that Arjuna must fulfill his duty in life, his dharma, and outlines the ideas that are at the basis of Hinduism involving Karma, rebirth and the goal of Nirvana. Action must be taken in the field of time in order to work out ones calling and challenges of a life well lived.

The Visconti-Sforza deck (fig.11, c.1450) displays a man with a large club about to strike a lion. This card and the rest that follow in this deck's trumps are clearly by a different artist than those that precede it. It represents a departure from the earlier Visconti deck, and the feminist ideals presented there. The man with the club is a reference to the Greek Hercules, a demigod and strongest man in the world. He was a person of extremes: too strong, too passionate, too single minded in his endeavors, usually carrying things too far. Hera, queen of the Olympian gods, drove him mad, causing him to kill his wife and children. He was then tested with twelve tasks in order to redeem himself. His courage is one of brute force. In one of those tasks he must enter Hades, which he does by killing Cerberus, the three headed dog that guards the entrance. This also references the character Pulcinella, of the "Punch and Judy" show, who kills his neighbor's dog and eventually defeats Satan with a club.

There is an earlier version of this card in the Visconti deck (fig.12) which displays a beautiful maiden with a crown and long golden hair seated on the back of a lion, opening its mouth with her hands. Her expression is calm and assured. This is clearly the opposite of the afore mentioned Visconti-Sforza deck; the figure with the club. It represents union and mastery over the beast's power through another means. It follows the feminist themes that run throughout these earliest cards we have, presenting skill, knowledge and expertise, in a more co-operative and accepting attitude of life. It calls to mind the tale of "Beauty and the Beast," most wonderfully brought to life in Jean Cocteau's film of the same name, illustrating the idea that in order to be lovable, one must first be loved.

The lion is the second companion beast we meet in the major trumps; the first being the Fool's dog. Like that animal and the others we will encounter on this journey through the cards, they represent the energies flowing from the unconscious elements of the psyche. This is the part of ourselves that Carl Jung asserted we cannot have direct knowledge of (unless you count dreams). It is hidden, just out of sight and so referred to as Shadow. Pamela Coleman-Smith, in the Waite-Smith deck, wonderfully extends this idea of companion beasts by adding cats, butterflies, snakes, fish, lizards, birds and more. Each can be seen as expressing a specific psychic energy emanating from the Shadow. Joseph Campbell talks about these forces as coming from the different organs of the body. "And if the body were not the soul, what is the soul?" Walt Whitman.

The two versions of this card present two separate attitudes that can be adopted to deal with these powerful influences. Without some method of understanding and channeling these beasts, we will become overrun. Does strength derive from an inner harmony or the force of will over these powers, or some of both. The lesson seems to be that in order to act effectively in the field of time, in society, we must encounter and have mastery over our inner self; this unconscious Shadow Self. This is not exactly what Freud labeled the "Id," mostly instincts, the urge to survive and propagate, but all that we inherited from millions of years of evolution, the body wisdom, and those experiences we bury in the unconscious. And, I would add, it is the playful, child self, that was our sense of wonder at this world, now left forgotten in adulthood. To reconcile ourselves with these energies, is a source of great power, vitality and creativity. Ignore these inner beasts and they can devour our life's energy. The Visconti deck, with the woman seated on the back of the lion, seems to be playing for an accepting, conciliatory model. Strength to act in the world comes from our inner center, and employs those powers from deep within us.

THE WHEEL: PRUDENCE

13. Wheel, Visconti-Sforza (c.1450)

So Yahweh said to Satan, "where have you been?"
"Round the earth" he answered, "roaming about."
So Yahweh asked him, "Did you notice my servant Job? There is no one
like him on earth, a sound and honest man who fears God and shuns evil."
"Yes," said Satan, "but Job is not God fearing for nothing, is he? … Stretch out your hand
and lay a finger on his possessions, I warn you, he will curse you to your face."
"Very well" Yahweh said to Satan, "all he has is in your power…"

Book of Job

The Wheel of Fortune was an extremely popular image during the Middle Ages. It turns up in illuminated manuscripts, churches and stories from the times. In one such tale King Arthur dreams he is placed atop a large wheel by a beautiful woman. She asks him what he sees and his reply is "the entire world." She then pushes him to the ground to remind him that earthly pride always comes to a fall.

This card is associated with the virtue Prudence: the word coming from the Latin, pruden, meaning foreseeing, wise. This may be a reference to the three Moiraes that spin the thread of man's destiny: Clotho, the spinner, Lachesis, the measurer, and Atropos, the cutter. The idea of the spinning wheel used to create yarn was seen as an act of magic by many in early times. In the "Sleeping Beauty" fairy tale, it is a spindle used in the spinning of thread that triggers the curse of 100 years of sleep.

This card usually shows a large wheel with men and women being raised up or rotated down on the wheel; often with a blindfolded woman turning it. An old man is at the bottom in the Visconti-Sforza (fig.13) version.

There is a relationship to this turning wheel and the turning of the four seasons. The suit of Wands, I believe, is closest to this idea, being the suit representing the farming class in Medieval society. They were dependent on and closest to the effects of the seasons. Their lives and livelihood depended on it. The idea of working the soil, farming, is an example of the "Grounding Experience" and is extended to all crafts that deal with raw materials from the earth: clay, wood, fiber, herbs and plants. When we work to create something out of these base elements, we are working with the principals that govern them. The material itself dictates what it can become. We must listen and work to reveal the essence within. Sculptors sometimes talk about working to reveal the form hidden within the stone. The art of craft is in infusing oneself into the process of creation, but in order to achieve that we must get our hands dirty: involve ourselves in the "Prima Materia."

In fairy tales this grounding experience takes the form of doing service, such as cooking, cleaning, tending the flock, gardening or some supportive menial tasks. Hansel and Gretel, Snow White, Cinderella all explore this element. In the Sleeping Beauty story, the curse put on Beauty is extended to the whole castle because the King, in an attempt to protect his daughter, outlaws spinning throughout the kingdom. This only serves to bring that fate to everyone, instead of just the princess.

This grounding experience is involvement in the turning of the wheel, the stuff of life which is sometimes painful, sometimes joyous and often messy. We do not control how the wheel turns. Prudence consists of memories, intelligence and foresight, and the willing participation in this movement, which is like the turning of the season. We become willing participants in the flow of life and open to what it presents us with; both good and bad. We accept what the Fates send our way on our journey.

TEMPERANCE: THE ALCHEMIST

14. Temperance, Visconti-Sforza (c.1450)

There was a time when everything was sacred. Making a well-crafted tool was a holy act. Using that tool was the enactment of a ritual. Our lives were connected to every mountain, tree and stone, all of which held the "anima mundi," the living soul of the world, the divine in nature. The natural world was alive and vibrant. Today, we find ourselves in a Cartesian reality, "I think therefore I am." This edict of Descartes' declares us separate from everything, including our bodies. We find the Ego, consciousness, alone trapped inside this body, somehow an alien in our own flesh, and the natural world as completely foreign.

The Temperance card is called the alchemist's card. It is an attempt to extract spirit from matter: to make holy that which is profane and reunite these two realms. To the Medieval mind matter was not inanimate but held the spark of life within. They were aware, even before the translated books from the great Mosque at Toledo began filtering into Europe, of Aristotle's four elements: earth, air, fire and water. All things both living and not were said to be made of a mixture of these four elements.

The thinking went; if you take a seed and place it on the table, nothing will happen, but if you put that seed in the ground where it is exposed to all four elements, it will grow into a living plant. It was further reasoned that life was put into the seed from the matter it was exposed to. The four elements had the essence of life in them and infused it into the seed, which made it grow. This idea was called "the doctrine of divine emanation," and although it went against official Church thinking, crops up throughout the Middle Ages. The Valentinian Christians and the Adamites sects both saw this idea as the basis of their heretical belief systems. The divine put Himself into all the world and it is our task to realize it. This idea was also the basis for Gnostic Christianity: recognizing the divine in the world. But this involves making it "real;" working in and with the materials of this world. This is the purpose of ritual and the goal of craft.

This was the task of the Alchemist. The search for the "Philosopher's Stone" which, when added to a cauldron of molten lead, would turn it into gold. Gold was the realization of the Anima Mundi in matter. Producing it meant spiritual purity had been reached. The two realities were inseparable: the material and spiritual. The search to make gold was a quest for the soul of the world and the Self.

The Visconti-Sforza (fig.14) deck shows a young golden-haired woman, standing at the edge of a cliff, pouring liquid from one urn to another. She seems calm and serene, wearing a blue gown covered with golden stars. All other versions of the Temperance card bear the same basic elements. Waite has transformed the woman into an angel with glorious wings. The two chalices may have come from the Gnostic Christians' version of the Mass, from the first through the third century AD: one chalice representing Christ, and the other Achamoth, the Mother Goddess.

This card is the enactment of magic, which is not imposing one's will on the world but getting in tune with the rhythms and music of the universe. On its way to being born, the soul was said to fall through the seven spheres of the cosmos, each one holding one of the visible planets. The soul picked up the music that each had and that music is still in us but we have forgotten how to listen for it. Magic means involving oneself in a ritual act which brings together both matter and spirit: a mixture of the two to create a union. The alchemists invoked chemical processes to remove the husk of the world and reveal its soul, the kernel of life. The process put them in tune with the universe and its music.

The Temperance card speaks of this endeavor to reach the spiritual through the material. It is associated with the suit of cups, originally representing the clergy, and the search for the Grail: the sacred cup that can heal the Fisher King. This is one of the main stories that stood at the philosophical heart of Medieval society. In it, Percival, on his journey, finds the Grail King, with a wound that can only be healed if a he breaks the code of chivalry and asks "who does the Grail serve?" The quest is a metaphor for the individual's search for Self, and inevitably leads one into the "forest savage" to meet the dark aspects of who we are. Only by being lost can Percival find the Grail King's castle.

THE PLAY

Life is what happens while you're busy
Making other plans.

John Lennon

One day we awake to find we are an actor on a stage. We feel we belong there, but are not quite sure what the play is or who our character represents. The director is feeding us our lines and prompting us as to what to do and what actions to perform, but everything is strange and unfamiliar. The other actors seem to know what to say and do and gradually we are able to, more or less, fall into place. But we are never very comfortable with the situation; nothing seems real.

This is the stage of the Self and the play is our life. Each actor on the stage is part of who we are. Each has his or her own agenda, and our consciousness, the Ego, is just one of many participants vying for center stage. With time, we learn what motivated each actor and how the plot of our life is taking shape. We find allies and identify foes. We fight battles and accept aid and advice, but always there looms a dark specter with its own agenda, often working off stage. We cannot become the person we are meant to be without confronting this unknown form.

In dreams we experience the many actors of the Self, of which the Ego, the conscious idea we have of who we are, is only one. The Shadow Self never comes into the full light of the action on stage but works to move us in, sometimes, conflicting directions from our conscious intentions. It is the seat of the unconscious mind. This is not what George Lucas calls "The Dark Side," in the Star Wars movies; the embodiment of evil. It is, though, rooted in the body and, as such, is not concerned with conventional morality. Its focus is with the well-being of the Self, not necessarily that of the Ego. It houses the wisdom of the body and uses the language of symbols to get its message across. Jung's "archetypes" are the expression of this energy, which can be a well source of creativity and inspiration. The world's myths and fairy tales reflect these motifs of our personhood on a grand scale. They are our angels of intuition, feelings and insight. If these voices are not acknowledged, then those angels become our demons, plaguing and inhabiting our dreams.

From my experience, we all have an ally in the guise of, in men, the Amina, and in women, their Animus. The former is the feminine in men and the later, the male side of a woman. Carl Jung came up with these ideas, realizing we have garnered much from our parents that makes up our personality, which remains unconscious to us. Acknowledgement of this side of ourselves can give one much strength and guidance. It can be a great helper in dealing with shadow material, much as the giant's wife, in "Jack and the Bean Stalk" was for Jack, hiding him from her husband, the ogre.

As they say, "the show must go on," but whether we are in a comedy or tragedy is dependent on how well we understand and listen to other voices on that stage. The Fool, as an actor on our stage, can be a great ally. He reminds us that this play is, in all actuality, not of our design. We learn to become active in the action as it is, not what we think it should be.

The Vision Quest

All people, at one time or another, find themselves at a point in their lives, where the mundane, status quo existence is not fulfilling. It happens often when children reach adolescence, when relationships fail, when jobs become an empty grind, or when something in them begins to assert itself; something unrealized. Life then becomes "the waste land," barren and unfulfilling. This is Dorothy's situation in Kansas, in the beginning of the L. Frank Baum story, "The Wonderful Wizard of Oz." The 1939 Hollywood movie pointedly brings this home. Life should be fertile, filled with growth but has become a dust bowl, barren. The farm attempts to go on, but has been stifled; "This old incubator is gone and we're liable to lose all our chicks."

The movie does a beautiful job of representing this state of a life gone stagnant, with sepia tone starkness. This is where Dorothy's creative, intuitive side begins to assert itself. The "Id Trickster" as represented by Toto, is asserting itself. We all have this side to us which is where playfulness, art, music, literature, and the appreciation of nature come from. Our society does not seem to value this part of the Self, except in special circumstances. It is not given a prominent place and must be set outside of common life.

Elmira Gulch represents the, so called, "real world" view that wishes to put Dorothy under wraps, or rather, her dog Toto. Miss Gulch is powerful and has the Law (the force of society) on her side. She is Wall Street that cannot see beyond the bottom line. She is a life lived without depth or feeling, existing only on the surface. She represents evil.

Many in life allow the creative, intuitive, playful, trickster side of themselves to be locked away, living the life of surfaces, without real depth. It is no small thing to carry out the burden of the mundane and requires courage and fortitude to live out this existence. It is, as Thoreau said, a life lived in "quiet desperation." This is the existence represented by the Munchkins, who possess no real power over themselves or their situation. They live in rules and regulations ("but we've got to verify it legally"), at the mercy of those in power ("are you a good witch, or a bad witch").

Many live this life, but it is not for Dorothy and she is destined to take up the "Hero's Journey". She cannot simply "find a place where you won't get into any trouble". She longs to make real her vision and decides to go on a quest; over the rainbow.

When you step outside of the ordinary life and begin to travel down a road leading beyond the day to day, into a deeper existence, you tap into unconscious forces: archetypes that were there waiting, all along. Forces come alive and things begin to happen.

In the movie, Dorothy, as she runs away from home, crosses a bridge over a small stream. This is the first hint that life is possible: that there can be new growth. On the other side she meets the primordial Wise Man, who will guide her on her journey. It's interesting that Professor Marvel is a flimflam, a humbug, but it is a sad society that loses its wise men or women even if they are a bit of smoke and mirrors. He none the less, makes Dorothy realize what is truly important in life: the depth of relationships; her love of Aunt Em. However, there is no going back once you have crossed your "Rubicon." The energies of life, your internal life, have been set loose and embody the power of a cyclone, which could destroy you if unheeded. "You cannot go home," you must continue on your path.

Dorothy is now on the Fool's Journey where she must assimilate the three essential qualities or virtues: Knowledge, Passion and Courage. These she meets in the guise of the Scarecrow, Tin man, and Lion. She has ventured out of the civilized world and is gradually led into the Wilderness. The path becomes unsure, the way turns dark and nothing is certain. The golden path, Yellow Brick Road, is sometimes hidden or blocked. Many a writer or artist throws down the pen or brush at this point, feeling lost or overwhelmed. It is only by virtue of Knowledge of the craft (the Scarecrow), Passion for the art (Tin Man) and Courage (the Lion) to be who you have begun to be, that can see one through. And Toto is there through it all, sometimes leading you astray, sometimes making discoveries, sometimes adding confusion, but always bringing forward the playful trickster energies of the Self. I see the Ruby Slippers (silver shoes in the book) as representing the passion (red) for the way to the jewel of the Self. This is no easy road we are on.

Only after the four Virtue cards have been encountered and woven into the fabric of one's life can the challenge of meeting the Shadow Self be pursued. This is Dorothy's acceptance of her three friends and they, making her journey theirs: the Scarecrow as the clear vision of Justice, The Tin man as devotion to the turning of The Wheel of Fortune, whatever the cost, and the Lion as Strength, courageous action. Temperance should be fulfilled in the person of the Wizard, but Baum expresses, in the story, that this virtue is only fulfilled by meeting inner truth head on. Dorothy must go to the Witches' castle herself. This echoes the Greek legend of Theseus entering the labyrinth. He is given the magical thread by Ariadne so he can find his way out. Dorothy has the good Witches' blessing as a kiss on her forehead, which is why the winged monkeys don't harm her despite the wicked Witches command.

In traditional Hindu society, this stage of life, the Vision Quest, comes at the very end. The man gives up all worldly concerns, family, work and friends and walks off into the forest to enter a meditative life. The hippies in the 1960s attempted this quest in their youth, rejecting the materialistic life society was offering them. The use of drugs, particularly LSD, was thought to be an instant pathway into the Vision Quest. It did not have the transformative success originally hoped for, though it did remove the "emerald tinted glass" locked on by society, at least for a time. These revolutionaries did begin one wise course, they opened the door to the east and its wisdom. They sought their Virgil to lead them through the underworld. They met the Hermit.

THE HERMIT

14b. Hermit, Visconti-Sforza (c.1450)

14c. Hermit, Waite (c.1909)

Midway in our life's journey,
I went astray from the straight road and awoke
to find myself alone in a dark wood.
Dante "The Divine Comedy"

The Hermit card was originally called simply "time.' The Visconti-Sforza (fig.14b) deck shows a man with a long white beard wearing a two-tiered hat, standing with a staff in one hand and an hour glass in the other. There is the burden of time on him, but he is far from broken. This is another transitional card standing between the Virtue cards and the Dark cards. It represents moving from a time when most of life's energies are spent on things external, the mundane, to a looking inward; a time of contemplation. For many this can happen

34

in the form of a "midlife crisis." The goals and expectations we had in our twenties never panned out. The sure path is lost and we are in the proverbial woods, surrounded by unknown dangers.

The Hermit card is leading us to the "vision quest." Starting with the Marseille deck the card is given its current name and connotes the idea of wise council. The hour glass has become a lantern. Waite's deck (fig.14c) further illudes to this theme of a guide though dark times. His figure is tall and strong with the lamp held high, calling out to lost souls.

Ironically the Hermit leads us not back to a safe secure life, but further into darkness. Like Virgil leading Dante through hell, he guides us to meet the darkest part of our soul. These elements must be dealt with before we can lead a fully human life. This is Luke Skywalker entering the cave to meet Darth Vader, who, unmasked, has Luke's own face. This is Theseus in the labyrinth and Dorothy in the dark wood before she is captured by the Wicked Witch of the West. Theseus has Ariadne's magic thread and Dorothy has her friends, the Lion, Scarecrow, the Tin Man, and Toto, who is her trickster self that prompted her to begin the journey in the first place. Luke has the guidance of Yoda and Obi-Wan Kenobi.

A curious thing occurs in some of the male hero's journey. The protagonist is helped by a mother figure, or wise woman. Jack, of the Bean Stalk, is hidden from the Ogre in an oven by the Ogre's wife. Gilgamesh is given advice by Siduri on what the good life entails and is warned by the Scorpion's wife that he must traverse the tunnel to the other world before the sun sets or he'll be burnt up. He is further aided by Utnapishtim's wife, being told where he can find a plant that restores youth. Dante's second guide, after Virgil, is Beatrice, leading him onto purgatory and eventually heaven. Whatever the gender, the Hermit is someone who guides us on our path. This could of course be a specific person but could also be a book, poem, piece of music or a gentle walk alone in the woods; some person or event that leads us deeper into the Self.

The Fool has traveled from the domain of parents, teachers, and elders, meeting the Empress, High Priestess, Emperor, and Pope, in the development of Ego. Then integrating that Ego, the sense of self, into the world through the four virtues: Justice, Courage (or Strength), Prudence (the Wheel), and Temperance. The Magician propels him or her on their way, and with luck, they will have experienced the love of someone to give their all to (the Lovers card). Now having met the Hermit, they are prepared to enter the labyrinth. The next four cards are the "dark cards" and represent meeting the Shadow. This will be the Fool's greatest challenge and presents many dangers. It ultimately means relinquishing a hold on the world of work, obligations and schedules, not necessarily in a literal sense, but adopting a focus on a deeper meaning and learning to bring that experience into daily life: an awareness of our Shadow.

I have hinted at this part of the psyche when talking about the Fool's dog; his companion animal. But this side of who we are gets forgotten after youth and is buried deep inside, out of sight.

This part of us is intuitive, based in the body. We experience energies bubbling up to the surface of consciousness as emotions and dreams. Some few find connection early on to this part of themselves, perhaps in art, theatre or music, but most of us have hidden it away and try to ignore its' influence. We have created the Minotaur ourselves and locked him away. Now, in order to live a fully human life, we must enter those dark regions and confront that part of who we are. It is Freud's Id, but also memories and experiences we could not deal with throughout our life. It is neither good or evil, but is originally nature; our essential nature, but neglected. Carl Jung confronted this part of himself in "The Red Book." The writing of it gave him power over it, so its consuming energy could be harnessed. He then went on to do extensive study and writing about Alchemy.

I have mentioned that the Tarot is not a philosophical treatise but offers practical guidance for daily living. The practice of a daily readings for oneself and developing a time and basic ritual with the cards, can be a meditation on the energies from within and without that are driving our lives and can give one mastery over them. This is the point of the Vision Quest.

THE HANGED MAN

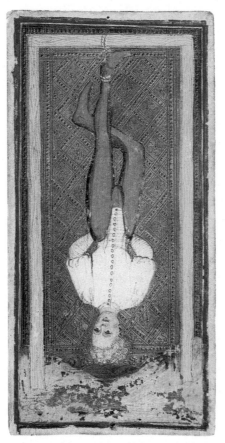

15. Hanged Man, Visconti-Sforza (c.1450)

This card (fig.15) was originally called "The Traitor." Apparently, this was the way traitors were dealt with in the fifteenth century: hung by one foot, upside down. It must have been a particularly nasty way to die. Some versions of this card also show two bags of silver on the ground; a reference to Judas Iscariot who betrayed Jesus for thirty pieces of silver and hung himself after realizing what he had done.

Every day Ego consciousness betrays us. It declares, "I am all, and master of everything." It is the source of all fear and desire. It is not our true reality and must be sacrificed; given up as the focus of the mind. This is what is behind the Hindu idea of Maya: the word literally meaning, "that which is, but is not." It is what the Buddha transcended when he meditated under the Bodhi tree. It is Jesus, forty days in the dessert. Both were tested by dark forces, as were Dionysus and Odin, both hung from a tree. It is the exchange of the mundane for the spiritual and at its essence is the call of sacrifice.

36

Arthur Waite and Pamela Colman-Smith, along with many writers, actors, and artists of late 19th century England, were members of a secret society, The Golden Dawn. They enacted a ceremony for initiates that involved binding and suspending them in air for a time. This seems to be a direct reference to the Hanged Man card. The experience was actual as well as symbolic.

In the movie "My Dinner with Andre," Andre, who is rambling to his friend Wally about his recent journeys, relates that he has had a breakdown and traveled to a forest in Poland and then to the Sahara dessert with a Japanese monk and finally went through a mock funeral, being buried in a grave to be uncovered and brought into a rebirth celebration. Andre admits he has no idea what he was doing. He is lost and the old familiar world he used to inhabit no longer makes sense. The movie ends with a long discussion about how we are all just going through the motions of living, rarely, if ever, touching what it really means to be alive. Andre is on his "vision quest" but still feels unfulfilled. He and Wally are both actors and Andre's searching and exercises seem a bit artificial, more like theatre than life. Wally, on the other hand, argues that he is alive in his little daily rituals, enjoying the small good fortunes he finds there, even though life is a struggle. Perhaps the quest is accomplished through life, not outside of it. In this we are reminded of Siduri's advice to Gilgamesh, "Savor your food, make each of your days a delight, bathe and anoint yourself, wear bright clothes that are sparkling clean, let music and dancing fill your house, love the child who holds you by the hand and give your wife pleasure in your embrace. That is the best way for a man to live."

In the early 1100s, Peter Abelard began teaching at the university of Paris. He came up with a revolutionary idea that went against Church teaching. The Church preached the "Doctrine of Ransom" which stated that Christ had to live and then die on the cross to pay for Adam's sin, Original Sin, that we all share in, before heaven would be open to mankind. Abelard, on the other hand, claimed that God, being omnipotent, could have forgiven that sin at any time and Christ becoming man was an act of pure love. His suffering and crucifixion were out of supreme generosity that we might, in turn, love God more completely. Jesus as the Hanged Man expresses that act.

None of the "Hanged Man" cards I have ever seen show someone in pain and suffering. Waite's version shows a man transfixed in bliss. If this card is about sacrifice of the Ego that we have established and integrated into the world, then it is out of love for life and the world, not contempt for it, that it is sacrificed. This seems at the essence of the Buddha's teachings: compassion for the world and those who suffer in it; escape from the misery of the world, and the illusion that the Ego creates, causing both desire and fear. The sacrifice of this part of ourselves is to enter the state of Bliss. When Joseph Campbell says, "follow your Bliss," it is not a call to be happy, but a challenge to burn with passion for a depth to life that goes beyond our consumer-based society.

DEATH

16. Death, Visconti (c. 1441)

The Devil card is flanked on either side by two cards of cataclysmic circumstances. The first of these is the Death card. The Visconti version (fig16) of this card is a skeleton riding a horse holding a scythe in the act of harvesting several persons below him. There are children, a cleric and people of both low and high birth. This speaks to the idea that this event comes to all, much like the "Wheel of Fortune" displays persons of all stations in life being turned 'round. No one can avoid the outcome of death. The Visconti-Sforza deck (c. 1450) displays simply a skeleton with a large bow in one hand and an arrow in the other. He seems to be gazing out at us.

This card is often given the interpretation as not being about actual physical death, but about change occurring in one's life before we can grow to full humanity. I agree with this idea in essence: you cannot face the Shadow Self until the ego is stripped bare. Day to day living must give way to a deeper meaning, and a recognition that our inner and outer reality is filled with wonders we only barely perceive. But consider the fact that death was real and ever present in the times these cards were invented. The 1300s of Europe saw famine, plague, and the Hundred Years War. What we think of as a simple curable injury could maim or kill. Life was short, hard, and unbelievably cruel by modern standards.

Starting in the early 1400s, images of the "Death Macabre" began appearing in churches, manuscripts and plays. A skeleton, Death, was shown taking an individual by the hand and leading them out of this life and into the next. Like in the earliest version of this card, the Visconti, people of all walks of life are subject to this fate, but the people in the Dance Macabre are walking along with death, not being harvested by a scythe. The move to the next phase is made on one's own feet, being led by the hand. It is a willing act in life, not just an inevitable consequence.

This is reminiscent of the morality plays being performed in the Middle Ages. These were the story of the "Everyman" being called by Death and the Everyman's attempt to find a companion to walk this road into the next life with him. The other characters of the play represent vices and virtues a person cultivates in life. None but "Good Works" is willing to accompany the Everyman in his quest.

A mock variation of this play still exists in the form of the "Punch and Judy Show" done with puppets. In it, the character Punch, commits murder and is hung but eventually triumphs through brute force, even against the Devil. This follows the Hercules motif; taking things too far, and letting passion rule. Punch's first transgression is to kill his neighbor's dog who is annoying him with its barking. His reaction is extreme and only escalates from there.

The Death card, as seen from the perspective of the modern Tarot, is about giving up the Ego as the center piece of life, and its view of the world as separate and controllable through the conscious self. The idea of the Ego comes from Freud, who believed it sat between the Superego, the norms of civilized life and the Id, pure instinct derived from the body. The Ego part of the Self was left to choose its actions from these two opposing sides. Carl Jung, Freud's student for a time, seemed to believe the Id, or unconscious self, is much more than just the "mindless primitive." He believed it held a wisdom that could be harnessed. Alan Watts and eastern philosophy in general seemed to see the Ego as imaginary; a fiction needing to be eliminated so nature and life can be experienced directly, without the judging, categorizing and editing of our experiences. Theirs is the mantra: "Be here now." If the Ego is a fiction, it is a persistent one. Perhaps the east sees the Ego as unnecessary because so much of life in that culture, at least traditionally, is focused on one's duty to society; the individual comes a distant second. We have based our society on "life, liberty, and the pursuit of happiness." The individual is the primary concern here.

The alchemists saw the world as the husk of reality that had to be purged in order to reach the kernel of existence. Throughout life we focus on our conscious thoughts of what life should be. Our challenge is to stop the noise and listen to a deeper Self; the one speaking in our dreams and at quiet moments in our lives, experiencing nature, listening to music or viewing a work of art.

The Death card throws off the Ego's perspective, for a deeper view, but like in the "Death Macabre" we must be ready to dance as it takes us by the hand. It is sometimes sad, sometimes celebratory, and it often takes us by surprise without warning, which is the message of our next card, "The Tower."

THE TOWER

17. Tower, Marseille (c. 1550)

    Both the Tower and the Devil cards are absent from the Visconti and Visconti-Sforza decks, the earliest sets we have from the 1400s. Perhaps they did not exist or were hidden for fear of the Inquisition. Modern decks place the Tower on the other side of the Devil card from Death. It usually has a tall structure being struck by lightning, with people falling to the ground (fig.17). It is, in the words of the theologian Paul Tillich, "a shaking of the foundations;" when all we know and trust, crumbles for some uncontrollable circumstance. It is we who are falling from the structures we have built to maintain our lives. This situation is the Alchemist's fire, burning off the impurities of the world, to reveal the gold of existence. In Greek mythology, it is Demeter putting the child Demophon into the fire to burn off her humanity and make her immortal. This can manifest itself as a descent into a deep depression that leaves one crushed by the burden of existence, or the sudden shock of a totally unexpected circumstance entering our life. This is the long barren winter, waiting for the cock's crow, awakening us to a new spring. It is the coming of old age, extinguishing the fire of youth and leaving us in a dark wood.

In the 1996 film "Box of Moonlight," John Turturro plays Al Fountain, the foreman of a construction project that is ended unexpectedly. He uses the break to take time to explore an area of the country he once knew as a child. He runs into, almost literally, a young man, Buck (the Kid), who is living on the fringes of society; "off the grid." Al gets entangled in the Kid's life, which eventually challenges all Al's assumptions about the way he lives his life. Buck is a bit of a thief and definitely plays the character of the Fool. This acts as a lightning bolt, shocking Al out of what he took to be a "normal life," and changing him forever.

Clowns, who play act this part of the Fool, often wore a head dress that can be seen as a cock's comb. The cock wakes up those sleeping; so too the Fool opens our eyes to the reality we often sleepwalk through. It is a sad society that loses the Clowns and Fools who can jolt us out of the mundane into a deeper reality. We live comfortably in the cage we build to protect us in life. The Tower card rattles the bars and throws open the door, leaving a new world open to us. Do we step out into the unknown or remain in our safe domain?

The Magician, being the Fool who has been through life's journey, is the trickster who also shakes us out of the sleepwalk we often enact as a substitute for a full vital life. His call can be painful but is often needed before we can meet our darkest side: The Devil.

THE DEVIL

18. Devil, Marseille (c. 1550)

"Which road leads to the Wicked Witch of the West?" asked Dorothy.
"There is no road," answered the Guardian of the Gates;
"no one ever wishes to go that way."
"How, then, are we to find her?" inquired the girl.
"That will be easy," replied the man; "for when she knows you are in the land of the
Country of the Winkies she will find you, and make you all her slaves."
L. Frank Baum, "The Wonderful Wizard of Oz"

The Devil (fig.18) is the winter of the soul and is the force that captures all our energy and binds us in
anger, depression, envy, hopelessness, fear and alienation. This is the dark hibernation that listens for spring's

promise of new life. This is the labyrinth where we hide our fears and failings, sacrificing our creative playful selves once known in youth. We have put this beast here and chained ourselves to him. It is a Minotaur of our own making. But it wasn't always this way. Once we walked hand in hand through the forest of our dreams. We danced with Pan and celebrated our nature.

When the early Christians encountered the worship of Pan, they interpreted him as the Devil, Satan. To these followers of Christ, the body and the whole world had been corrupted by the sin of Adam and only by imitating the life of Jesus and receiving the sacraments administered by the Church, could one be saved. Pan was a god of nature and fertility, also the patron of flocks and goat herders. From waist down he was goat. But he was also a god of music followed by nymphs into the forest for nights of dancing revelry. For the early Christians this represented the epitome of sin. Salvation lay in restraining the natural impulses of the body, not celebrating them.

We have inherited this attitude and lost the spirit that Pan originally represented to the Greeks. We have repressed and silenced the soul of nature and replaced this playful attitude for a life of phone calls, schedules and obligations. In the film, "My Dinner with Andre," Wally, on his way to meet Andre, laments that, in his youth, he once thought about art, music and theater in New York, were he grew up and still loves; now all he thinks about is money. Pan's influence is no more than an occasional memory, or sometimes a dream.

Fairy tales often deal with this repressed aspect of the self, that is a product of living in a society that does not acknowledge the nature we have hidden away. With no outlet to express these energies, ogres, giants, and witches begin to inhabit the unconscious mind. If unheeded, these forces capture our life's energies and drain the joy and wonder that life was as a child. These demons threaten to devour us, if we have not prepared the soul to endure this long dark season; the dormancy of the soul.

One of my favorite fairy tales concerning an encounter with the dark mysteries of the Self, is the Russian version of Cinderella; Vasilisa. She is tricked by her stepsisters into going to see Baba Yaga, a powerful witch who lives in the forest in a house on chicken legs. She must restore the light her sisters have intentionally put out. Baba Yaga tells Vasilisa to perform certain tasks while she is gone for the day and if she returns with the chores unfulfilled, she will eat the girl for a meal. This happens three times, and on each occasion, Vasilisa succeeds with the help of a doll her deceased mother gave her. We dare not enter the dark without some form of aid in our Quest.

In the Waite-Smith version of this card, a naked man and woman are chained around the neck to a block that the Devil sits on. The chains are loose and could easily be removed by themselves. Perhaps this expresses the idea that this season must be endured until the time is right. We wait for spring's bugle call to awaken us from this night of the soul.

If this card had been designed in Asia, I could imagine the figure of the Devil as being the Dragon. It, in the tradition of the East, is the spirit and force of nature and its power to renew itself after winter. Unlike in the West, dragons are not hunted down and slain but celebrated. In our culture they demand gold and young maidens, two things they have no use for. They are not a source of power but a being to be feared and eliminated. Have we poisoned the well spring of our nature? The Devil card is the facing of the Shadow Self; our hidden self that only appears to us in dreams but can rule our lives if unheeded.

L. Frank Baum's Dorothy, like Theseus, Jack and many other heroes in our lexicon, kills the confronting evil. I am proposing that this darkness has been made evil by our neglect of its calling. I believe an alliance can be made to integrate it into life. It is, as Jung perceived, the source of living creativity. In the movie "Harold and Maude," Harold spends his time going to funerals, where he meets Maude, also a funeral goer. After they team up and witness a building demolition, Harold's idea, Maude asks, "Is it enough?" She states that she loves to see things grow. Life is all around. They eventually transplant a tree from a city street to a forest as an act of affirming this sentiment.

The Devil card is synonymous with the seed being planted in the ground. In the mind of Medieval peoples, and the period these cards were invented, the four elements, earth, air, fire, and water, where infused with the life of the universe: the Anima Mundi. The seed was not simply dormant but actively absorbing this life force. The Darkness does not stifle growth but is a part of it.

This brings me back to the idea of the Grounding Experience: time spent captured by Shadow, but which also connects us to these elemental forces of life. In the brilliant animated film by Miyazaki, "Spirited Away," young Chihiro is moving with her mother and father to a new town. They get lost in a wooded area, after her father decides to take a short cut. They then stumble onto a long-deserted amusement park, where they find booths filled with wonderful food prepared and just waiting for them. It's actually a place where the spirits come to renew and refresh themselves, and because the mother and the father have eaten the food meant for these spirits, they are turned into pigs, slated to be slaughtered. Chihiro must save her family by becoming a worker at the bath house in the town, run by Yubaba, a powerful witch. She must scrub and clean the baths and floors and attend to the guest spirits. Master Haku and Lin help the young girl in her effort. Because of Chihiro's good heart and, with the aid of her new found friends, she eventually triumphs.

Whether it is Cinderella, the Goose Girl, Iron John, Dorothy or Chihiro, all must work through the dark by performing some seemingly menial task: cooking, cleaning, gardening. This is symbolic of the Grounding Experience, which involves getting in touch with the stuff of life: wood, fire, clay, fiber. In so doing, we are getting in touch with ourselves, if the work is performed as a sacred act: a collaboration between the living material of life and the artist themselves. We pour who we are into the craft of our hands, and this is what harnesses the Darkness for our benefit.

JUDGEMENT

19. Judgement, Visconti (c.1441)

This card was originally titled "The Angel," showing one or more winged cherub blowing a long horn. Below are naked people rising from a crypt. At the top of the Visconti (fig.19) version of this card, the oldest example we have, are the words, written in Latin, "Rise for Judgement." This is clearly a reference to the Christian's last day, when Christ returns to judge the life we have led determining where we are to dwell for the rest of eternity. The Egyptians also had a myth of final judgement where the heart of each soul was weighed on a scale against that of a feather by the goddess Maat, who represented harmony and order in society and the universe. Apparently, the goal of life in their society was to make light your heart and not weigh it down with misdeeds which could have disastrous consequences for society at large.

From a modern perspective, this is the Ego waking to a new reality. We move from being captured by our Shadow, our unconscious self, to a state where those elements of the psyche begin to integrate into daily life, and no longer control our fate. This is the last of the transitional cards: moving from the darkness to cosmic light, connecting our consciousness to all the universe and its life. I have placed it here, rather than in its traditional sequence, number 20 in most decks, to show it as a movement from the Dark cards to the Astral cards; the last four in the major arcanum.

If, as I and many others who study the cards believe, these images were designed to preserve an approach to life that would have been heretical to the Church, then this card speaks more to the here and now than to a future event. The Taborites, Adamites, Picards of Bohemia and others sects of the Late Gothic period in Europe, as far as we can tell from the scant evidence left behind, believed in realizing the Kingdom of Heaven here on earth. It was the idea that all matter, living or not, contained the spark of the Divine and could be realized through communal works and ritual. Judgement, and the call of the Angel's horn, was a waking to this truth. That call, out of darkness, is often a sudden jarring moment announced like the morning cock's crow, rousing all to the new day. It was the Fool in spring, who played this part in Medieval society, usually acted out in the festivals during this season. It is his energy that revives the earth each year, ending the long dark of winter.

In ancient Greece the myth of Demeter's search for her abducted daughter, Persephone, who has been taken by Hades to live as the Queen of the underworld, dramatizes the flow of the seasons in story. Upon hearing of the events of her daughter's kidnap, Demeter, goddess of the harvest, is so distraught that nothing grows on earth, threatening to destroy mankind. In one version of the story, as she searches the world for her daughter, she comes to Eleusis where the king, Celeus, employs her as wet nurse for the infant prince. The queen, Metanira, recognizes her nobility and offers her a resting place and drink. This Demeter refuses in her grief until Pan and Echo make her laugh with their antics and jokes. It is their foolery that breaks the spell of utter desolation. Zeus then send Hermes to retrieve Persephone, but because she has eaten a pomegranate seed, she must spend one quarter of the year in the Underworld with Hades: thus, we have winter.

This story is very similar to a Japanese myth about the sun goddess, Amaterasu. She hides in a cave, refusing to shine on the world because of an argument with her brother, bringing darkness to the world. The gods try to get her to come out and save humankind, using cymbals, flutes and even a cock's crow. Nothing works until they hang a mirror on a tree and begin laughing. When Amaterasu comes to the mouth of the cave to see what is going on, the gods call out that a new god has arrived even more beautiful than she. Stepping out of the cave she sees herself in the mirror and is then grabbed by the "Strong Armed Man of Heaven" and put back in the sky. The Sun is restored to her rightful place in the sky by mischief and play.

The Fool assaults our mundane perception of the world by invading our consciousness with mischief and playfulness, with no regard for decorum. One of my favorite masters of clowning is Harpo Marx. He wonderfully executes the fool's character throughout the Marx Brother's films. In "Monkey Business," towards the end of the movie, as the four brothers, who have stowed away on a ship, are attempting to go through customs, each trying to impersonate a legitimate passenger, Harpo enters and starts flinging the paper forms up in the air: total chaos ensues. He is the master of mayhem. Like the Greek god Pan, another trouble maker, Harpo is also a master musician. From my experience, playfulness and music have a lot in common. It is even called "playing" an instrument.

From this awakening we can begin to approach the last four cards: the Astral cards. This is when our work becomes the act of integrating the Shadow Self into the real world. From the Vision Quest we have developed a relationship and dialog with the hidden parts of ourselves and must now bring that knowledge into society through our craft. This is what the Alchemists called the "Great Work." It always involves the Grounding Experience; working with the elemental stuff of life: Earth, Air, Fire and Water. This is the Bodhisattva's work here on earth, born out of compassion. Its' what fairytales express when the heroine is put into service of the witch. This is Demeter as the wet nurse to the young prince, on her search for her daughter, and our quest in the search for wholeness.

THE STAR

20.Star,Viscoti(c.1441)

21.Star,Marseille(c.1550)

According to the oldest version of this card, the Visconti deck (fig.20), this is the card that represented Hope. It's the third of the divine virtues to appear and depicts a crowned woman, with hands folded, gazing towards a glowing light, a star, in the upper right corner of the card. Her wrists are bound by a cord which is connected to an anchor at the other end. The image of the anchor was symbolic of the Catholic Church. This motif seems to signify that she is bound by its Law. Beneath her is a man crouching with a cord around his neck. Apparently, at one time, the words, "Juda Traitor" were visible on his garments. This is no longer seen. Each of the divine virtues in this deck, has a version of a man beneath the feet of a female figure, as if to say, Faith, Hope and Charity, the three Divine Virtues, will triumph over worldly ways, but its meaning is not at all clear.

The Star as a card of hope represents following the light into the night to find fulfillment. It brings to mind the "Star of David" leading the wise men of the east to the manger of the Christ child. The Marseille deck's Star (fig.21), shows a naked woman pouring the contents of two urns onto the earth and a pool of water respectively. She is nourishing both elements here on earth. I am struck by the feminine aspect of this card and the grace she bestows on one who is on the path. Theseus, Gilgamesh, and Jack are all aided by a woman on their quest. Perhaps we are dealing here with Jung's Anima in men: the solace and guidance derived from the feminine.

In the fairy tale Rapunzel, the heroine is forfeited by her mother for taking rampions, a type of onion, from a witch's garden. The daughter is forced to live alone in a tower, having contact only with the witch, until a prince discovers the secret and begins visiting the girl himself using her golden hair to climb the tower. After the witch finds out about the transgression, she blinds the prince, who is then forced to wander the forest in darkness. Rapunzel tricks her captor, the witch, escaping to go in search of her lover. In some versions, on the journey she gives birth to two children, a boy and a girl. After finding the prince, it is her tears that give him back his sight. To me this tale portrays the essence of the Star card: seeking your fulfillment, bliss, through connecting your life to another's, and being willing to fight for it. It is through the other that you find wholeness.

This story also brings up the elements that seem to run throughout the female "Hero's Journey." Hers is a Quest that connects one person to another, has a period of being captured by the Dark (the witch), relies on cunning and the help of others to be liberated from this force and often involves the "Grounding Experience," working with the elemental stuff of life often in the service of others, for example Cinderella or Vasilisa. The male "Hero's Journey" is usually a solitary quest often involving brute force to achieve its goal. The knight kills the dragon, while the woman serves and outwits the witch. Both quests are legitimate, but if you look at the cards of the Visconti deck (c. 1441), I believe it is making a strong case for the feminine version. This is the deck that has a woman knight in each suit along with the male. It may also be why the Grail Quest legends of the Middle Ages are so elusive for Arthur's knights to fulfill. Finding the Grail is not simply a matter of vanquishing a foe, but demands breaking with the code of Knighthood and asking "Who does the Grail serve?" It turns out engaging in a battle is much easier.

I am presenting this card as the first method of bringing the experience of Shadow into the landscape of daily life. Following the Star is to bind one's life to another's. This harkens back to The Lovers card, which is an experience crowned in innocence. Following one's Star, on the other hand, is the work of a life matured though experience. Ironically, shadow is created by light and so remains mostly a mystery; can never be fully illuminated. But the Ego can recognize and acknowledge the Shadow and connect with it. Rapunzel was captured by the dark, in the witch's tower, but escapes into the light to search for her lover, her Star.

After one has made a connection to the Shadow Self, represented by the dark cards, the challenge is to bring that experience into daily life and allow this part of ourselves a voice in the light of living: recognize what our dreams have been telling us all along and making that truth real. The Star card achieves this through union with another and letting them be our light through the darkness. We follow a path that is uncertain with only one star, our love, to lead us on.

THE MOON

22. Moon, Marseille (c. 1550)

The Moon is the domain of the unconscious and harkens back to the High Priestess card. She is the mother holding the mystery of life. Her emblem is the moon that illuminates the world in shadow. Her light is reflected like a pool of water, and like water, is a symbol of the unconscious where another life takes place only dimly perceived by the eyes of consciousness.

In the Marseilles (fig.22) deck we see this pool with a crab, or crayfish, coming out of the water, and a dog and wolf at either side of a path that leads on into the night. A pale moon shines overhead with flecks of light falling to earth. In Medieval times it was thought that the dew descended from the moon. So, her influence covered the earth at night. But that influence waxes and wanes. It reflects the cycles of nature and those of a woman's body.

In George MacDonald's fairy tale, "The Day Boy and the Night Girl," written in the late 19th century, a golden age for such stories, a witch, Watho, raises a boy who she keeps in ignorance of the night and a girl who knows only night and is kept in an underground room with only one glowing lamp. When the girl's lamp unexpectedly goes out, she gropes her way up to a garden with the full moon shining down. She is overwhelmed by its beauty and thinks this moon must be the mother of all lamps. Upon venturing into the garden on different occasions she sees the moon in various phases and concludes it must grow and then die to grow again to an even greater brilliance.

The Moon card represents the second motif of dealing with the Shadow Self in life. It is the domain of the "hero thief;" one who takes inspiration, insight and energy from the realm of the unconscious but does not integrate it into daily living, and so remains in this half-light of the moon. This is Prometheus who steals fire from the gods, Jack who takes the giants three treasures, and Theseus who kills the Minotaur in the heart of the labyrinth. In taking from the dark, without exercising mastery over their foe, they put themselves in the position of being constantly pursued by shadow. Things do not end well for these heroes, despite the wealth they have garnered from the wellspring of the unconscious. I see many artists and writers follow this path, some to disastrous ends. Jackson Pollack, Jack Kerouac, Aleister Crowley, and Sylvia Plath may be a few modern examples.

The influence of the moon is not a sure path. It sometimes leads one into total darkness. The wolf and dog in the Marseille's Moon, represent the fear of nature. Following this scenario we are cut off from the "body wisdom:" that voice that knows the path we should follow. Creatures from the depths we have ignored, plague our dreams at night and thoughts during the day, despite the power we have gained from the moon's reflected light. We must take up the sword and vanquish the dragon of our own creating. The hero thief becomes the warrior knight and does battle daily.

The only alternative to this state of affairs is to name the beast, and gain control over it. Like the girl in the fairy tale Rumpelstiltskin, naming the adversary prevents him from stealing the gold back and gives you power over him. Learning the true name of the shadow allows an alliance of sorts. Power must be exercised to command this element of the Self or it will steal the child of creativity. The working of one's craft and exercising a command of the elements to produce something of value for the community, is the act of "naming."

Isis created a snake to bite and poison the god Ra. In pain he called to Isis to heal him but she would only agree if he told her his true name. His response was: Khepri at dawn, Ra at midday, and Atum at evening. She said he still had not revealed his true name so Ra told her in secret. We must discover our soul's secret true name.

THE SUN

23. Sun, Marseille (c. 1550)

24. Sun, Waite-Smith (1909)

This is the full light of the intellect and is the domain of conscious reason and will. This is Apollo, god of prophecy, poetry, music and the healing arts. The card represents the disciplines that seek to understand the world through the construction of a lens that views life from one specific point of view. Philosophy, religion, science, all represent an image of truth, but each from a specific perspective. Religion asks, "what is the Supreme Being's plan for us?" Philosophy asks, "how can human life have meaning?" Science asks, "can the puzzle of the universe be solved and what are its basic governing principles?" They each seek truth but ask very different questions, and view it from different perspectives.

In Medieval times, it was thought that the "walled garden" was the ideal relationship mankind could have to nature: a world set within the constructs of civilization and tended to, bringing forth fruit. Nature, but not the wild abyss of the forest. The word "paradise" comes from a Persian word meaning a walled orchard. The garden is a product of nature, but cared for by man.

In the Marseille (fig.23) deck we see two nearly naked youths, standing under a glowing sun with flecks of light floating down. Behind them is a brick wall. The idea here is a return to a state of innocence, protected behind a constructed barrier, basking in the full light of day. This is the state within the walled garden, symbolic of the intellect and reason of the mind: the discipline that accepts certain precepts or axioms as reality, such as the belief in a god or that pure reason can reveal truth, or that the mysteries of the universe can be solved and reduced to mathematical formulas. The enactment of the discipline is an act of ritual, and within these accepted ideas we can enter the wonder that is the world, fully as a child in innocent delight. This is not simply going through the motions, but letting ourselves become transported by the astonishment of it all. The act of ritual becomes a sacrament. We enter a state of bliss within the walls of our intellectual constructs. This sometimes becomes overwhelming as in the case of the mystics, like St. Francis of Assisi, or the poet Walt Whitman or the artist Van Gogh. In this state we burn with the mystery from without and within. Even Einstein declared that "a sense of wonder" was the beginning of true science. It is the state of being transported by music, art, literature or Nature itself.

In Ray Bradbury's book, "Fahrenheit 451," Guy Montag escapes a society where all books are outlawed and burnt, to find refuge in a community of people who keep books alive by memorizing each one and then teaching it to another of the group. They are secluded from the "civilized" world so they can pursue their love of literature and the truths revealed within. Books and learning are their Sun and they have walled off the world to fully engage in their devotion.

In the Waite-Smith (fig.24) deck, we have a naked child holding a flowing banner riding bare back on a white horse. The wall is seen behind with large sun flowers growing under a brilliant sun. This companion beast, the white horse, is a creature that can transport this child self, even though there are no reins. This is the Shadow transformed from darkness to full light and occupies a cooperative relationship to the Ego, the Self, a child, basking in the bliss of life. This state depends on establishing this walled garden where nature is allowed to grow while being carefully tended. I believe this is where all true spontaneity, art and creativity lie, and is the lesson of the Sun card.

The Companion Beast has been transformed from the Fool's trickster dog, to a lion being gently controlled, in the strength card, to now a beast fully living in an equal state with the conscious Self. We have made full circle to a union with our Shadow Self, that we once walked hand in hand with as children. We are ready to enter the World, renewed.

THE WORLD

25. World, Viscoti (c.1441)

The final card of the Major Arcanum is the World and represents fulfillment in the sense of finding one's place in the community. This is the domain of the hands, giving expression to our inner selves through craft. Pottery, fiber arts, woodworking, gardening all involve putting ourselves into the world through a medium. Working the four elements and perhaps, quite literally, getting our hands dirty; performing every act as sacred. Our Shadow Self is expressed through the work of our hands.

Both the Waite-Smith and the Marseille decks show a naked woman dancing surrounded by the four Evangelists represented as a lion, a calf, an eagle and a man. These traditionally stand for the four apostles who were thought to have written the gospels of the New Testament: Matthew, Luke, Mark, and John. They can also be seen as these four elements, earth, air, fire, and water, in harmony revealing the gold of existence. The

"Anima Mundi," spirit in matter, is fully actualized. We are no longer tied to the movement of the Wheel of Fortune. Instead, we are dancing to the harmony of the spheres.

The Visconti-Sforza deck (c. 1450) displays an elaborate castle on an island with stars above. This is within a globe being held up by two naked cherubs standing in a green pasture. The oldest deck, the Visconti (fig.25, c. 1441), my absolute favorite, has a regal matron hovering on a scalloped edged cloud with a golden trumpet in her right hand and a crown in her left. She looks out at us as she floats over the scene of a seaside town with three ships sailing off from the shore. The Medieval town consists of four castle-like structures with a small river running through. In the foreground is a knight on horseback carrying a banner. Two monks in a boat are rowing up to meet this knight and on the far shore is a man kneeling on the bank, fishing in the river. There may be a halo around his head. One cannot help but think of the "Fisher King" legend and the knights from Arthur's court that ventured to find the Grail held at the Fisher King's castle. Percival's journey to find the Grail is the Vision Quest of the Ego to find wholeness, but a break with the protocol of chivalry must be made to heal the Fisher King and restore the land to its fertile state. "Who does the Grail serve?" It serves those who have met and reconciled themselves with their Shadow Self.

The female figure hovering above this scene is interpreted as "Mother Mary:" gracious queen of the Church, bestowing good on the earth. This deck's final image completes its feminine stance with the mother of the Savior embracing the earth and those people living in it.

It is important to remember that this World, if it is to bear fruit, relies on our work in it. Music, literature, all the arts and craft must have a connection to daily life, and an engagement with the "stuff of life." They are not merely intellectual exercises. The World card speaks to this co-operative relationship that engages our entire self with the world and gives back to it. It is the final and completing method of integrating the Shadow into every day existence. It is given expression through our creative work in the world. The idea of the Boddhisatva, in Buddhism, re-entering the life of the community out of compassion for the suffering of man, is at the heart of the World card.

In Chauvet, with its wonderful drawings of prehistoric animals on the cave walls, there is evidence of a ten-year old child exploring the underground cavern, five thousand years after the art was originally executed. Along with his or her foot prints are the prints of a wolf's. They follow the path of the child's prints and we don't know if this beast accompanied the child or was even there at the same time. I choose to think of this animal as the child's Companion Beast. We enter the depths of the soul and if we have developed a relationship with our Shadow Self, it will accompany us on our journey. We are not alone but only have this dark part of ourselves as an ally if we've been on the Vision Quest into our hidden mind; the Unconscious Self. The challenge is then to bring that experience back out into the world and make it real, giving back to the community. The World card is the fulfillment of the quest with the work of our hands.

I think the early humans must have existed much of the time in a state of "Dream Time," much like young children who see no separation from the world and themselves. Thus, the world is infused with their life. Chauvet and Lascaux were cathedrals to this mentality. Cro-Magnons were not trying to gain power over the animals they depicted, but celebrate their power as existing in themselves. They were the world they perceived. To perform our work in the world is to put our Self into the lives of others, and make it real.

Practical

The use of the cards should be practiced on at least a semi-regular basis. There are many spreads to choose from once you've chosen a deck that appeals to you. (Decks with 78 cards will be of the traditional type, with four suits and 22 trumps as discussed in this book.) In the beginning, though, it is best to keep things simple. Pulling one card a day and using it as a focus for meditation throughout the day may be best. A personal ritual should be developed each time you do a reading, beginning with a few minutes to center your thoughts and then the shuffling of the deck. Lighting a candle or soft music or whatever appeals to you, should be done regularly so it becomes a cue to your mind that you are now entering something outside of daily life. This is a time to focus on deeper matters, where feelings and intuitions take the lead.

My favorite spread is just three cards drawn at random and I use it not as a past, present, future reading but more of a snapshot of life right now: the forces that are influencing my present situation. I'm sometimes asked, "What if the cards just don't apply to me at all?" This is almost never the case because the themes running throughout the Tarot are universal; archetypes. They usually present something of relevance to anyone seeking answers to the mystery that is life. Readings are always about you, and dive deep into the motivations that are influencing you from within and without. We should be aware, though, that many of the problems we encounter out in the world are caused by projections we throw on to it. We really do make the world from our own consciousness, and much of that mind lies in shadow; unconscious to our Ego self. Knowing that dark part of ourself is the point of the practice of the cards.

Do not read cards reversed. Each card will have negative and positive energy and will manifest that side of itself depending on you and the position it comes up in. You need to be in touch with your feelings and intuitions about a particular card at that moment. The traditional meaning of a card is secondary to how the images strike you right now. This comes with much practice but yields many rewards as you make the cards personal. Remember, you are writing your narrative; this is your story. The journey you are on is one only you can tell.

It is helpful, after you have laid out the cards and given them a few moments to settle in your mind, to describe, in your own words, what you see in each card. Is the figure male or female? Are they on the move or settled? Are there companion beasts present? What role do they play? Do any of the cards represent an ally; are any of them obstacles? You could make up your own list of questions about how to view each card. The Tarot presents life as a tale of the journey of the Fool from innocence to enlightenment. We are that traveler, creating our narrative on the road to a deeper existence. Let us begin to be the master story teller we were born to be.